THE EMPIRE INSIDE

The Empire Inside

Indian Commodities

IN

Victorian Domestic Novels

SUZANNE DALY

THE UNIVERSITY OF MICHIGAN PRESS   ANN ARBOR

2014   2013   2012   2011   4   3   2   1

A CIP catalog record for this book is available from the British Library.

Library of Congress Cataloging-in-Publication Data

Daly, Suzanne.
    The empire inside : Indian commodities in Victorian domestic
novels / Suzanne Daly.
        p.   cm.
    Includes bibliographical references and index.
    ISBN 978-0-472-07134-0 (cloth : alk. paper) — ISBN 978-0-472-
05134-2 (pbk. : alk. paper)
    1. English fiction—19th century—History and criticism.
2. Domestic fiction, English—History and criticism.   3. Commercial
products in literature.   4. Material culture in literature.   5. Middle
class in literature.   6. Imperialism in literature.   7. India—In
literature.   8. Material culture—Great Britain—History—19th
century.   9. National characteristics, English—History—19th
century.   I. Title.
PR878.M38E67   2011
823'.8093553—dc22   2010024621

Acknowledgments

Earlier versions or portions of three chapters were published previously. Chapter 1 appeared in *Victorian Literature and Culture* 30, no. 1 (March 2002), under the title "Kashmir Shawls in Mid-Victorian Novels," and is reprinted here by permission of Cambridge University Press. A portion of chapter 2 was published in *Victorian Studies* 50 (winter 2008), as "Spinning Cotton: Domestic and Industrial Novels," and appears by permission of Indiana University Press. Chapter 3 appeared in *Nineteenth Century Studies* 19 (2005) as "Indiscreet Jewels: The Eustace Diamonds." I am grateful to the editors of these journals for their permission to publish these chapters in their present form.

Contents

Introduction:
Colonial Commodities and the
Naturalization of Empire

Have you Indian curiosities? I thought they were only for ladies?
—Charlotte Yonge, *The Clever Woman of the Family*

Charles Dickens's *Our Mutual Friend,* a novel deeply committed to making moral connections between the home and the world of commerce, begins and ends with invocations of infants, the issue of a corrupt and a virtuous couple respectively. Chapter 2 introduces Mr. and Mrs. Veneering, ambitious social climbers whose fall into bankruptcy at the novel's end parallels the restoration of John Rokesmith/Harmon to his family money. In addition to their "bran-new house in a bran-new quarter of London," complete with new furniture, friends, servants, plate, carriage, horses, and pictures, the Veneerings have a "bran-new baby"[1] to complete the scene. This nameless Baby is nothing more than an empty sign of its parents' unimaginative and unscrupulous acquisitiveness, a trait exemplified by Veneering's purchase of a seat in Parliament for £5,000 and his subsequent "over-jobb[ing] his jobberies," for which he is at last forced to resign.[2] Conversely, Dickens concludes the story of John Rokesmith/Harmon's disciplining of and marriage to the formerly grasping Bella Wilfer by rewarding the couple with wealth and a child.

The symmetry of these babies, small images of the two sets of parents who in turn are each other's mirror opposite, is disrupted by a third infant: the "Hindoo baby in a bottle"[3] who resides in Mr. Venus's shop.

Floating in its liquid grave, this small corpse, subjected to none of the sentimentalizing with which Dickens generally treats the infant dead, may be read in several ways. It is a neatly contained refraction of the larger bodies that Gaffer Hexam pulls out of that larger body of water, the Thames, for pay. It serves also to mark the stillborn romantic ambitions of Mr. Venus, the articulator of bones, and is referred to as "his own Hindoo baby."[4] But this "Indian baby," along with its shelfmate, "African ditto," cannot, once so labeled, be just a baby. It is a "Hindoo,"[5] but it is also an object bottled for display and a commodity for sale in a shop. Writing on what she calls the density of objects, Annette Weiner posits

> a continuum along which objects may be ranked according to their symbolic densities. At one end of the continuum are inalienable possessions—objects that should be kept within the closed context of family, clan, dynasty, or corporation, for example. Other, less prized possessions vary in their symbolic densities and, therefore, in their degree of interchangeability. Like commodities, things at the other end of the continuum without much symbolic density are exchangeable merely in terms of the value of their replaceability . . . [but] symbolic densities differ radically even with objects that are physically alike.[6]

Weiner here opposes symbolic density and interchangeability, but qualifies the opposition by claiming that even "objects that are physically alike" may possess different symbolic densities. In using this example I do not wish to suggest that the baby is in any way interchangeable with other things exactly like it; rather, interchangeability in this context means exchangeability. That is to say that as a commodity, the preserved corpse is exchangeable for money (Marx's universal equivalent), yet the majority of human corpses in Victorian culture were symbolically dense in that they were understood both legally and socially to possess claims on the living to treat them appropriately, which are here specifically denied. Stripped of its symbolic density as a human being in this setting, neither exactly a person nor a thing, although it approaches the status of both, the Hindoo baby thus occupies a unique place in the domestic novel, in which India is everywhere represented, but rarely by fully realized Indian characters.[7] Rather, the complicated and evolving relationship of England to India is mediated in novels through the relationship of English people to what were understood to be Indian things. The baby in the bottle may thus be seen to reference the ongoing effort to fix the colonies through the production of scientific knowledge even as it speaks to the need simultaneously to control and profit from a place frequently described in the press and in Parliament as uniquely uncontrollable and unprofitable—a nation, as Ranajit Guha has noted, understood to be without history, in its infancy.[8] The transmogrification of the dead body of an Indian infant into a commodity is also, of course, a profound act of dehumanization, a refusal of the social meaning of its death,[9] which suggests in turn the need to disembody those Indians living under British rule even as it makes literal the fantasy of being able at once to contain, control, and understand British India in a way that so complex and contingent an entity could never be. Finally, the "Hindoo" baby in the bottle figures synecdochically something that the British called "India" itself, just as the African baby represents Africa in some sense. Making Indian things, which may be owned without complications or ramifications, stand in for India thus works to create the illusion of absolute possession of a geographically dispersed, politically volatile, and still contested set of territories.

In his seminal essay "Modernism and Imperialism," Fredric Jameson observes that by the late nineteenth century,

> colonialism means that a significant structural segment of the economic system as a whole is now located elsewhere, beyond the metropolis, outside of the daily life and existential experience of the home country, in colonies over the water whose own life experience and life world—very different from that of the imperial power—remains unknown and unimaginable for the subjects of the imperial power, whatever social class they may belong to. Such spatial disjunction has as its immediate consequence the inability to grasp the way the system functions as a whole. . . . Daily life and existential experience in the metropolis . . . which is necessarily the very content of the national literature itself, can now no longer be grasped immanently; it no longer has its meaning, its deeper reason for being, within itself.[10]

Jameson's insights may be said to build upon Raymond Williams's thesis in *The Country and the City* that urbanization affected nineteenth-century novelists' ability to create "knowable communities"[11] that are themselves inevitably structured by exclusions. Jameson is careful to explain that he is leaving imperial adventure tales out of the discussion and is concerned only with central or canonical Modernist literature, in which he observes a "systematic block on any adequate consciousness of the structure of the imperial system."[12] I wish to argue that this block is everywhere evident in mid-Victorian literature, and that Indian commodities function as the political unconscious of the text in the Jamesonian sense, regularly gesturing at what is just off the page. Furthermore, the erratic relationship of these representations of things to the world of commerce—unquestionably commodities, they are most frequently portrayed in novels as gifts, possessions, and household goods—bespeaks a conflicted sense of the role India plays in the world of British commerce and finance.

To speak of "India" as a stable or ontologically coherent entity, however, would be an anachronism, and mid-Victorian newspapers and magazines registered this fact regularly. Military engagement punctuated the nineteenth century as England expanded its holdings in South Asia, and myths of absolute dominion were thus culturally necessary to mark an imagined outcome as well as an imaginary present. This book finds meaning in the histories of three entwined phenomena: the nineteenth-century history of Indian commodities that had a significant effect on Great Britain either economically or culturally; the history of territorial acquisition in this period that impacted the production and flow of these commodities; and the commodities' ubiquity in so-called domestic literature.

Bill Brown has used the term *material unconscious* to describe "literature's repository of disparate and fragmented, unevenly developed, even contradictory images of the material everyday." According to Brown, a "materialist hermeneutic seeks to retrieve . . . images not as the historical context that explains (away) the idiosyncratic details of the literary artifact but as a historical text that relations between such details allow us to write."[13] Much excellent work has been done on the British *in India* that shows how nineteenth-century domestic culture was affected by England's engagements there, and this book is animated by and deeply indebted to these studies.[14] More recently, scholars of history and literature have taken up the relationship between the British Empire and English culture from the standpoint of the metropole.[15] My aim in examining the British at home and in looking specifically at material objects is to work out the implications of the argument that in making something called "India," the English also remade themselves. I do so by resorting to Brown's notion of the historical text as intertext: India should not be made to function merely as the backdrop to a narrative of English national identity. Rather, while England's imperial ambitions in India are integral to an understanding of Victorian literature and culture, India is central to the story, not merely the occasion for someone else's narrative. I therefore read the images that the English constructed of themselves at home, from home, as part of a dialectic; while ideas and beliefs about India-as-colony that circulated widely in Victorian England were a significant part of the discursive field utilized by novelists who appear on the surface to concern themselves solely with England and Englishness, the history of the British occupation of India, I argue, subtends these mystifications and must be brought to light in order to comprehend them fully. Material histories give us glimpses of human histories, stories of exploitation and agency that the novels will not tell but cannot leave alone either. India is thus woven deeply into the texture of English domesticity, but in such a way as to need unraveling at this remove. Things that Victorians understood to concern or be "about" India, in other words, are intimately present if not immediately apparent. Furthermore, as Elaine Freedgood has noted, our reading practices themselves militate against paying attention to objects.

In *The Ideas in Things: Fugitive Meaning in the Victorian Novel,* Freedgood observes that while "the Victorian novel describes, catalogs, quantifies, and in general showers us with things . . . we have learned to understand them as largely meaningless: the protocols for reading the realist novel have long focused us on subjects and plots; they have implicitly enjoined us *not* to interpret many or most of its objects."[16] Freedgood describes the manner in which objects are thus "lightly read" as "weak metonymy": objects merely "suggest, or reinforce, something we already know about the subjects who use them."[17] Objects, she argues, must be followed off the page in order to understand how "the knowledge that is stockpiled in these things bears on the grisly specifics of conflicts and conquests that a culture can neither regularly acknowledge nor permanently destroy if it is going to be able to count on its own history to know itself and realize a future."[18] In this reading, representations of objects in novels occupy a medial position in the cultural imaginary; objects stand between history and memory, for they contain traces of that which the nation can neither confirm nor deny but must hide from itself because this knowledge cannot be done away with.

Similarly for Brown, recourse to the history of objects opens the possibility for more perfectly comprehending the culture that produces the art in which things are named with such insistent regularity. In *A Sense of Things: The Object Matter of American Literature,* Brown has argued that paying close attention to material culture in literature allows us to see "how we use objects to make meaning, to make or re-make ourselves, to organize our anxieties and affections, to sublimate our fears and shape our fantasies."[19] In the Anglo-Indian context, I would argue, these issues are equally compelling, but my answers to these inherently psychoanalytic queries turn us back toward the materiality of the thing, the history of its production, sale, and consumption. This book, then, examines the ways in which Victorian novels offer readers ways to make sense of emerging notions of both British India and the British home through the medium of Indian imports, but it does so by attending to the material histories of mythologized things. I take up their movement through the intricate and unevenly developed spaces of the colonial enterprise, and into the homes in which novelists unfailingly enshrine them, to argue that these fictional imports mediate culturally the very idea of imperialism, just as actual imports mediated and stood in for the multifarious processes of colonial wealth extraction. In *Rule of Darkness,* Patrick Brantlinger argues that a key purpose of Victorian imperialist doctrine was to weld together or disguise the contradictions inherent in the goals of "military conquest and rapacious economic exploitation [and] idealistic although nonetheless authoritarian schemes of cultural domination."[20] Military action, he suggests, was often explained away by the expediencies of the "civilizing mission," but commerce was a harder sell; it "generally seemed antithetical to heroism and high ideals."[21] Yet a central term in nineteenth-century imperial discourse labors mightily to undo that contradiction: the idea of "industry," both as a Christian virtue to be imparted to the "natives" and as the motor of the barely hidden economic agenda behind the Christianizing, civilizing, or reformist doctrines of the imperial enterprise. Will to industry serves as a counterpoint to Brantlinger's insight that class difference in England both remains in place and is externalized onto colonial subjects over and against an anachronistic (to the degree that it is not totally phantasmatic) "Englishness." How, I want to ask, is Englishness shored up by a particular brand of commodity fetishism that turns goods produced in British India into emblems of English identity?

Faced with the idea that colonial India was in some ill-defined way connected to, if not a part of, their nation, English novelists helped to domesticate and contain the *idea* of India by writing Indian imports into the novels as indispensable accoutrements of middle-class English life. In so doing, they provide a powerful demonstration of the ways in which the economic imperatives of imperialism shaped the English imaginary from the inside.[22] At the same time, as the novels appear to consolidate the role of women in an emerging model of private life wherein they make meaning inside the home, Indian commodities connect middle-class women to the economic, cultural, and military work of empire building even as actual women are being evacuated from the realm of economic productivity.[23] The four constellations of commodities on which I focus—Kashmir shawls, cotton textiles, tea, and gemstones, particularly diamonds—are all strongly identified with women, although in profoundly different ways. While in Britain the material culture of India inevitably suggests or refers to India on some level, Indian things may work in several possibly contradictory registers at once: at different moments, they may speak to English class aspirations, gender, morality, or national identity even as they gesture obliquely at their place of origin.

In *A Sense of Things,* Brown argues that scholars and theorists of material culture must necessarily confront "the indeterminate ontology where things seem slightly human and humans seem slightly thing-like";[24] this study locates such indeterminacy in a form of fetishism that imbues foreign goods with both human and mythical, "Oriental" attributes while allowing these attributes to stand in for the labor that is congealed (if not embodied) in them. Brown further cautions that even "as the prose fiction of the nineteenth century represents and variously registers the way commodity relations came to saturate everyday life, so too . . . this fiction demonstrates that the human investment in the physical object world, and the mutual constitution of human subject and inanimate object, can hardly be reduced to those relations."[25] My aim is not to reduce the study of colonial material culture to commodity relations but to explore the colonial commodity form in detail as a crucial part of the trajectory of these objects' existence that in turn reveals the ways that the costly British desire for Indian territory and wealth was justified and popularized through a range of costly and desirable commodities. Nevertheless, *The Empire Inside* registers and analyzes numerous moments at which inanimate objects are made to come to life and "speak," although such speaking almost invariably tells a story about their English possessors. But commodities cannot speak for themselves; in attempting to speak for them I hope to shed light on the ways that their fictional counterparts are made to mean.

The desirability of Indian commodities was not promulgated solely through the novel. Throughout the mid-Victorian period, periodicals aimed at both middle- and working-class readerships were consistently and overtly concerned not only to describe the geography, history, and politics of India but to explain the origins of the imported goods that ordinary Britons might own or wish to own. Novels and magazines make use of the same Indian commodities to sell copies, but they rarely do so for the same purposes: magazines played up the "exotic" origins of colonial goods, while novels tended to occlude those origins. Yet most of the novelists in this study were deeply involved in magazine journalism: Charles Dickens was, perhaps most famously, the founder of *Household Words* and *All the Year Round;* Elizabeth Gaskell wrote for Dickens and published most of her novels in serial form; Mary Elizabeth Braddon edited *Belgravia;* Margaret Oliphant wrote for *Blackwood's Magazine;* Sheridan LeFanu edited the *Dublin University Magazine;* Anthony Trollope edited *St. Paul's Magazine* and founded the *Fortnightly Review.* As part of a continuum of print culture, magazines and novels do not represent the literal and the figurative; rather, each assists in the process of uncovering that which is implied or assumed in the other. Victorian journalism on India ranges from sober analyses of the political landscape to the more common travelogues that tend to read like expository passages from imperial adventure tales. Such essays as "Assam and the Hill Tribes," "A Visit to Cashmere, by a Captain in Her Majesty's Service," and "The Cotton Fields of India" are less interested in fact-finding than in mythmaking, and their success in this endeavor may be measured by the degree to which Indian exports retain the trace of the "Oriental" in the Victorian cultural imaginary.

To understand the role of Indian commodities in this imaginary it is useful to consider not just what the commodities do in the home but how they arrived there. This practice follows Arjun Appadurai's dictum that in order to understand fully the ways in which commodities affect culture and vice versa, it is necessary to "follow the things themselves, for their meanings are inscribed in their forms, their uses, and their trajectories."[26] In so doing, we begin to see how and why they were produced for export, information that Marx held to be occulted by commodity fetishism.[27] What emerges is a constellation of Indian industries that, while driven by Indian labor, were often founded and owned by the British themselves. Tracing what Appadurai terms the "social life" of Indian commodities leads us directly to concrete instances of phenomena that are too often spoken of in the abstract: ruralization, annexation, the widespread conversion of Indian workforces to wage labor, and what Byron Farwell has called Queen Victoria's "little wars," those wars of imperial expansion that are frequently forgotten in what we tend to think of as Victoria's largely peaceful reign.[28] It thus becomes clear that accounts of the Manchester textile industry (to give the most obvious example of an industry heavily represented in Victorian novels) are inadequate unless placed squarely in a colonial context.

As this context makes apparent, however, British rule in India was hardly a unified enterprise but rather was fraught with contradictions. Its goals, strategies, and outcomes were bitterly contested and divergently pursued, largely (until its dissolution in 1858) by the East India Company and the British regiments attached to it, but also by more or less independent capitalists who invested in colonial ventures; by missionaries; by colonial administrators in the field; and by cabinet members and bureaucrats in England. Details of these conflicts may be found in such contemporary sources as the *Times* of London and the Parliamentary Papers, but midcentury novelists rarely resort to imperial politics as plot devices: India appears only as deep background, the provider of things the provenance of which is neither explicated nor questioned.

Midcentury novels thus permit us to read more clearly the cultural work that colonial imports were doing within the realm of "the domestic," understood both as the household and the nation-state. (As Aamir Mufti and Ella Shohat have observed, "home" in this double meaning is the "verso to the recto of ideologies of imperial gregariousness.")[29] Social historians have argued that the nineteenth century saw the consolidation of the nonproductive household—that in which no yarn was spun, cheese made, poultry kept, and so forth. This shift was partly the result of the intertwined phenomena of urbanization and industrialization, partly the result of the (not unrelated) rise of the middle class and a concomitant shift in thinking about the nature of the middle-class home and the role of women within it.[30] Looking at Indian imports through the role they play in Victorian novels works to broaden an understanding of Victorian ideologies of both work and home as they intersect with the novel, and the facts of British intervention in India are indispensable to piecing together these belief systems. But in turning to historiography, we begin to see India as the English imagined it, or India not necessarily as it was, but as it was understood to be. Therefore, this project is as much about India as a dreamscape, a mirror, and the site of abjected identities as it is about India as a geographic or political entity; I attempt to demonstrate how the various, competing ideas of India that find their way into the novels were created and contested. Gayatri Chakravorty Spivak has written that in the nineteenth century, "Europe had consolidated itself as sovereign subject by defining its colonies as 'Others,' even as it constituted them, for purposes of administration and the expansion of markets, into programmed near-images of that very sovereign self";[31] that is to say that in the interests of wealth extraction, the British labored mightily to make certain aspects of India operate on British principles. At the same time, Teresa Hubel observes that in the colonial period if not beyond, "India's reality extends beyond its geographical presence. It has also an imaginative dimension. . . . The potential for appropriating India increases when it is recognized as the property of the imagination."[32] Reading between magazine journalism and domestic novels of the mid-Victorian period brings these competing visions of India into focus, revealing how uneven were the processes of consolidation and administration to which Spivak refers, as well as the management of image and reality with which Hubel is concerned. Novels and print journalism document the ways in which "foreign affairs" influenced or determined how Indian commodities were understood by the English people who bought, sold, used, wore, consumed, and thought and wrote about them and what was at stake in these understandings.

My central problematic, then, is grounded in the study of material culture as it intersects both art and commerce: at a moment when the systems that produced and distributed Indian commodities were in flux, why were certain of these things being enshrined in novels as objects of desire or markers of middle-class status? What kind of work were they doing, and what did they mean to the middle-class readers whose lives the novels both reflected and helped to structure? And how does the presence of commodities relate to the absence of Indian people in certain privileged forms of cultural production? Working out the ways in which different commodities functioned at specific moments to make multiple and contradictory meanings will, I contend, assist in ameliorating the universalizing tendencies in the words *English* and *Englishness* and at the same time give the lie to the novels' invocation of a static and conquered India. When in India, Indian material culture points us to the wildly varying responses to and effects of British rule; when in England, it works not so much to consolidate English identities as to fragment them, marking sometimes minute distinctions of taste, class, and income level in English society. The frequency with which this fragmenting occurs in domestic novels, and the regularity with which Indian goods were called upon to perform this work, speaks to the need simultaneously to engage with and to disavow the coming-into-being of the peculiar and contradictory historical configuration known as British India. *The Empire Inside* argues that examining these strands of imperial and cultural politics in relation to one another opens up new readings of canonical Victorian novels' relationship to India as not just a means of individual self-definition but as the ground on which a phantasmatic idea of India was both disseminated and undermined; the novels' gestures at the historicity of British India, however oblique, allow us to undo their hypostasizing of Indian commodities as timeless embodiments of cultural difference recuperated as British status symbols.

CHAPTER ONE

The Private Life of Things:
Kashmir Shawls

In a feverish stillness, the intimate recesses of the domestic space become sites for history's most intricate invasions. In that displacement, the border between home and world becomes confused; and, uncannily, the private and the public become part of each other, forcing upon us a vision that is as divided as it is disorienting.
                    —Homi K. Bhabha, "The World and the Home"

It is by their apparel that types of society first become known.
                    —Frantz Fanon, "Algeria Unveiled"

Cloth and clothing inevitably signify, but they do so in different ways in different times and places. When cloth or clothing made for a specific purpose in one cultural context begins to be produced as a commodity and is appropriated as fashion by a different culture, meanings reverberate on both sides of the transaction. In nineteenth-century England, shawls known as "Cashmere" became such an item, although shawls were unique in that they were both cloth and clothing, that is, a single piece of woven textile that was worn as a garment.[1] For this reason, they carried not only the class associations that all garments do, but resonances of various strands of romanticization associated with the "East" as well as the quasi-religious personification to which uncut cloth, particularly that of non-European origin, is often subject.[2] First associated in Europe with French noblewomen, the shawls became popular with English women by the 1820s, and by the 1840s, when shawls of many descriptions were worn by women across the social scale, Kashmir shawls, or at least the desire to own one, had been adopted by the prosperous middle class. Not surprisingly then, they are ubiquitous in the domestic novels of the time where they function at once as a marker of respectable English womanhood and as magical and mysterious "Oriental" garments. They are also a coveted gift that men returning from colonial service in India bestow upon their mothers and sisters in a move that symbolizes the fitting and desired conclusion to a man's career in India: coming home wealthy, bearing the spoils of the East even as he reenters domestic space. As an unsigned 1852 essay by Harriet Martineau in *Household Words* titled "Shawls" prescriptively states, "when son or grandson comes home from travel, far or near, his present is a new shawl" despite the fact that "the supply which arrives from Asia over bleak continents and wide oceans, can only be for the rich and great."[3]

While shawls generally remain in the background of the novels, they nevertheless punctuate the texts with enough regularity to make it worth asking what kind of cultural work they might be doing in these frequent if often unremarked-upon appearances. For if Kashmir shawls were taken for granted, they appear also to have been profoundly desired. How and why did Kashmir shawls come to such prominence in the midcentury popular imagination, and what did they mean to authors and readers? I hope to begin to answer these questions not by reading the glamour of cashmere (the wool) or Kashmir (the place) on their own terms, but rather by examining this moment of Kashmir shawls' prominence in literature alongside the history of their production and sale, and their earlier and differently coded representation in paintings.

As part of the midcentury material everyday, shawls were an immediate and potent marker of women's status, especially when the women were outside their homes. Thus in Elizabeth Gaskell's *Mary Barton,* a group of factory girls is described as wearing "the usual out-of-doors dress of that particular class of maidens; namely, a shawl,"[4] and when John Barton's sister-in-law Esther returns from voluntary exile to speak to her niece Mary, she puts off her prostitute's clothing and obtains from a pawnbroker's "a black silk bonnet, a printed gown, a plaid shawl, dirty and rather worn to be sure, but which had a sort of sanctity to the eyes of the street-walker."[5] Esther thus literally wraps herself in a mantle of rented respectability: Judith Walkowitz explains that "the dress codes of [Victorian] prostitutes . . . served as a way of advertising themselves and attracting male customers. Bonnetless, without shawls, they presented themselves 'in their figure' to passersby."[6] The vast majority of shawls in nineteenth-century England were of domestic manufacture, and so powerful was the Kashmir shawl as a signifier of social status, in novels as in society, that its appearance even on a woman who clearly bears all the marks of poverty and hard living might temporarily unsettle the system of class markers, at least in a context lacking skillful readers.

In Charlotte Brontë's 1853 novel *Villette*, a "coarse," dissolute Irish woman passes for "an English lady in reduced circumstances" and obtains employment as a governess in a respectable Belgian household by virtue of having in her possession "*a real Indian shawl*—'un véritable Cachemire' . . . the spell by which she struck a certain awe through the household."[7] Lucy Snowe, the genuine article (that is to say, the genuinely distressed Englishwoman) who replaces this Mrs. Sweeny, remarks, "I feel quite sure that without this 'Cachemire' she would not have kept her footing in the *pensionnat* for two days: by virtue of it, and it only, she maintained the same a month" despite her unfortunate habit of drinking whiskey in the nursery.[8] As a certifiable Englishwoman, Lucy can do what the Belgians cannot: immediately identify Mrs. Sweeny's name and accent as "Hibernicé" rather than "Anglicé," and place her as a possible "washerwoman" who has undoubtedly stolen her lace caps, ill-fitting silk dresses, and the "majestic drapery" with which she adorns her "broad shoulders."[9] As Andrew H. Miller points out in his study of the circulation of commodities in Thackeray's *Vanity Fair,* the anxiety over thieving servants prevalent in so many Victorian novels is less an anxiety about the loss of items that are useful or valuable in themselves than it is about the servants' appropriation of the coveted signifiers of their employers' social status and the subsequent possibility of their own upward social mobility, even if that mobility only means owning a milliner's shop (like Becky Sharp's erstwhile maid Fifine) or trading the washing of household laundry for the higher-status if barely less taxing duties of a governess.[10]

Brontë gives her heroine good reason to demonize her rival: not only has Lucy gained employment at Mrs. Sweeny's expense, but as a true (and truly) distressed English lady seeking employment abroad without so much as a letter of reference, she cannot afford to have the integrity of her kind undermined by such impostors. Like her literary predecessors in gothic novels, Lucy is in a terrifying and culturally untenable situation: she is a woman alone, lacking a home, a family, or indeed connections of any kind, and thus intensely vulnerable to attacks on her position and her integrity from other (foreign) women. In keeping with the novel's structural conceit of events occurring in threes, her next rival at school is the Parisian teacher, Zélie St. Pierre, and her ultimate struggle, against her employer and erstwhile ally Madame Beck, forms the novel's climax.[11] In these terms, Mrs. Sweeny and her shawl are unimportant except that they serve a structural and thematic purpose—Lucy could not simply walk into the *pensionnat* and be given the job because the reader must understand that Lucy is someone to whom nothing comes easily. And they serve to remind us, subtly, that this character deserves something better, because despite her appalling lack of luck, her bad fate, she is socially on a level with her godmother, Mrs. Bretton, a "middle-class, English gentlewoman," and with Madame Beck, both of whom wear Kashmir shawls.[12]

With shawls, then, the novel again gives us three of something for no apparent reason. And it could be argued that in a novel filled with details of dress and fabric—lace collars, watch-guards, Madame Beck's silent slippers, M. Paul's *paletot,* the trauma of wearing pink in public and the anonymous comfort of winter merino—the shawls neither deserve nor require more attention than any of the other domestic trifles that make up *Villette*'s backdrop. That, however, would miss the point that domestic trifles are central to what *Villette* has to say about the harsh realities of class and economic demarcations.[13] As Nicholas Dames has demonstrated, Lucy Snowe must learn to regulate her desires in every sphere of her life, and a not inconsiderable part of the grim pleasure she takes in dressing plainly comes from the same ascetic strain in her nature that causes her to lecture herself on the necessity of practicing "self-denial and economy . . . and steady exertion."[14] This self-exhortation occurs just as Lucy comes to the realization that the man she loves, Graham Bretton, is someone for whom women's appearance and social status matter a great deal, who "in appreciating the gem, could [not] forget its setting."[15] He instead requires a love object who possesses "the imprint of high cultivation, the consecration of careful and authoritative protection, the adjuncts that Fashion decrees, Wealth purchases, and Taste adjusts."[16] Lucy must always be close to what she cannot have for her story to accrue the poignancy Brontë intends. Being just outside the market for fashionable commodities means that Lucy herself is less marketable, that she cannot circulate herself as she might choose.

Whether Lucy actually wants such adjuncts herself or simply wants them not to matter remains an open question; her desires are finally less quantifiable than those of the burgeoning consumer culture that helped to produce the market for Kashmir shawls and their multifarious imitations. As Ellen Rosenman has noted, "The link between private life, commodities, and women gives novels a hybrid identity: they are part of high art and cultural critique but also work hand in glove with conduct books, fashion plates, and women's magazines to feed consumer desire."[17] In other words, the novel form will always fail to sustain any cultural critique to the degree that it falls into the trap of valorizing bourgeois consumer culture. It is instructive then to think about how the mid-Victorian novel's relation to the consumption of imperial commodities affects its ideological or political investments. Marx and Engels observe in "The Communist Manifesto" that "the bourgeoisie has through its exploitation of the world market given a cosmopolitan character to production and consumption in every country. . . . In place of the old wants, satisfied by the productions of the country, we find new wants, requiring for their satisfaction the products of distant lands and climes."[18] Regardless of whether the "old wants" were in fact so satisfied, this succinct formulation—the market creates the desire in the consumer—is generally not taken up by historians of fashion or art in their discussion of Kashmir shawls (which hover, then and now, somewhere between these two poles). Unlike Marx, who in the *Grundrisse* argues that production "produces the object of consumption, the manner of consumption, and the motive of consumption," these critics tend to see the intrinsic qualities of Indian textiles as themselves primarily constitutive, at least initially, of consumer desire.[19]

Historians' technical explanations of what the shawls were, however, are indispensable to any attempt to understand Kashmir shawls' hold on the nineteenth-century imagination. To begin with the history of fashion: in *The Art of Dress: Fashion in England and France, 1750–1820*, Aileen Ribeiro notes, "By the early nineteenth century, imitation cashmere shawls were being produced in Norwich, Paisley, and Edinburgh, either of cotton or silk mixed with wool, or very fine wool. . . . Nothing, however, could match the real cashmere shawls for lightness and warmth, and this preference is clearly marked in contemporary portraiture."[20] Here is a familiar conundrum: that the Indian shawls, woven from the undercoat of Kashmir goats, were of unmatched and apparently unmatchable fine-

ness and quality is virtually never disputed.[21] It can be argued that the
feverish pace of textile-manufacturing innovations in England during the
second half of the eighteenth century was predicated on the need to compete with the demand for high-quality Indian textiles.[22] Yet the purely
functional reasons for Kashmir shawls' precedence (lightness and
warmth) do not account for their ubiquity in paintings of fashionable
women, most notably those of the Empress Josephine.[23] Their virtues
alone, however incontestable, cannot explain the shawls' mystique. Furthermore, to read these paintings only as recording and not perpetuating
desire seems limiting at best. The most famous portraits of French noblewomen and their Kashmir shawls were painted by Jean-Auguste-Dominique Ingres; while the shawls are faithfully rendered in the more aus-
tere portraits like that of Madame Devauçay (1807), in those of the
Comtesse de Tournon (1812), Madame Philibert Rivière (ca. 1805) (fig. 1),
and Madame De Senonnes (ca. 1814) (fig. 2), among others, the shawls
contribute to what Robert Rosenblum has called "a hothouse ambiance
of dense and indolent luxury" (*Jean-Auguste-Dominique Ingres,* 108), thus
linking these portraits thematically with Ingres's *Grande Odalisque* (1814)
(fig. 3), whom Rosenblum calls "the most obsessively fascinating of Ingres's nudes . . . an idle creature of the harem" (104) who "reclines in
padded luxury, fondled by satins, silks, furs, and feathers" (107), and who
bears more than a passing resemblance to the printed description in *Villette* of *Cleopatra,* if not to the actual painting, identified as De Biefve's
Une Almée, on which the passage was based.[24] By the 1850s, when Ingres
painted *Madame Inès Moitessier* (1851 [fig. 4] and 1856), the shawls, which
Georges Vigne has noted "appear so frequently in [Ingres's] female portraits that they take on the character of an emblematic signature," are entirely absent.[25] Not only has fashion shifted to more ornate and wide-
skirted dresses that do not support the lines of large shawls as did Empire
gowns, but a status symbol has yet again been taken up by the upper
middle class just as the aristocracy that popularized the style has abandoned it.

The shawls worn by midcentury Englishwomen, although probably
not of a quality comparable to those so stunningly recorded by Ingres,
were undeniably both warm and light, as their association in novels with
domestic comfort as well as social status or fashion attests. Even this
seemingly prosaic statement of fact, however, is capable of being magically transformed into a fragment of Orientalist fantasy. A catalog article

Fig. 1. Jean-Auguste-Dominique Ingres, *Madame Rivière*. 1805. Oil on
canvas. Musée de Louvre, Paris, France. *(Image courtesy of Réunion des
Musées Nationaux / Art Resource, NY.)*

Fig. 2. Jean-Auguste-Dominique Ingres, *Madame de Senonnes*. 1814. Oil
on canvas. Musée des Beaux Arts, Nantes, France. *(Image courtesy of
Réunion des Musées Nationaux / Art Resource, NY.)*

Fig. 3. Jean-Auguste-Dominique Ingres, *Grand Odalisque.* 1814. Oil on canvas. Musée de Louvre, Paris, France. *(Image courtesy of Réunion des Musées Nationaux / Art Resource, NY.)*

by Sarah Buie Pauley from a 1975 exhibition of Kashmir shawls at the Yale University Art Gallery quotes the Italian Jesuit missionary Ippolito Desideri's *Account of Tibet, 1712–1727.*

> Most precious and magnificent are the cloths called *scial* in both Hindustan and Persian. These *scials* are cloaks which envelop the head while the ends fall on either side of the body; thus the head, neck, shoulders, arms, breast, the back till below the hips and nearly to the knees are protected. These cloaks are so fine, delicate and soft that though very wide and long they can be folded into so small a space as almost to be hidden in a closed hand.[26]

Although any finely spun and woven wool can be folded into a small space, clearly the claim that a properly folded Kashmir shawl may be concealed in the palm of one's hand is not only an exaggeration but one with a familiar provenance. In the story of "Prince Ahmed and the Fairy Peri-Banou" in the *Arabian Nights,* the prince is given a magical tent that shrinks or expands as needed. Oddly enough, Charlotte Brontë also uses this tale in *Villette* to suggest the nature of Lucy's unrequited love for Graham Bretton.

Fig. 4. Jean-Auguste-Dominique Ingres, *Madame Inès Moitessier*. 1851. Oil on canvas. Samuel H. Kress Collection, National Gallery of Art, Washington, DC. *(Image courtesy of the Board of Trustees, National Gallery of Art, Washington.)*

I kept a place for him, too—a place of which I never took the measure, either by rule or compass: I think it was like the tent of Peri-Banou. All my life long I carried it folded in the hollow of my hand—yet, released from that hold and constriction, I know not but its innate capacity for expanse might have magnified it into a tabernacle for a host.[27]

While the *Arabian Nights* were perhaps less familiar to twentieth-century writers than they were to those of the nineteenth century, the fact that the very people who had the materials on hand to try the experiment apparently failed to realize that they were telling a version of a fairy tale that had been extant in Europe since the first years of the eighteenth century gives some indication of the sort of mythologizing impulse to which Kashmir shawls seem always to have been subject.[28] And Brontë's weaving of Oriental tales and cashmere into *Villette* is hardly coincidental; she knew the stories of the *Arabian Nights* well, and she not only refers to them explicitly at least ten times in the course of the novel,[29] but she appropriates, for this story of a homeless twenty-three-year-old in a foreign country, their sense of obscure and potent forces at work that might at any moment deliver up the unexpected. Thus the familiar contrivances and coincidences of the mid-Victorian novel are overlaid with a frisson of the unknowable that, as Brontë astutely realizes, can no longer be extracted from the worn-out conventions of the gothic. In the dangerously Catholic world of the convent/school, gothic trappings abound but are simultaneously skewered: the "mysterious" ghost-nun, before our very eyes, lights a cigar and falls out of a tree before being revealed to be nothing more than Ginevra Fanshawe's lover in disguise. The *Arabian Nights* offers fresher opportunities for Brontë to breathe a suggestion of the supernatural into *Villette,* and like the Bible, Romantic poetry, and the work of Sir Walter Scott, it is central to Brontë's own idiom.[30] *Villette* is a tale full of genies, fairies, elves, and magic lamps, and placed in this context, Mrs. Sweeny's shawl does perform a kind of transformative magic, however brief the duration of its effects.

Further evidence of Brontë's association of Kashmir shawls with both respectable English womanhood and Oriental magic occurs in the moments when English men "play" with them. This play occurs both in *Jane Eyre* and *Villette;* in *Jane Eyre,* Rochester acts in a pantomime "costumed in shawls, with a turban on his head . . . [looking] the very model of an eastern emir," thus simultaneously retaining some relationship to his identity as lord and master of Thornfield and the most powerful man in the room, and making a piquant contrast to his habitual state of English manliness.[31] In *Villette,* conversely, Graham Bretton is the unwitting object of a prank that his mother plays on him as he sleeps. As she tells Lucy in a letter,

> I took it into my head to play him a trick: so I brought out the sky-blue turban, and handling it and him with gingerly precaution, I managed to invest his brows with this grand adornment. I assure you it did not at all misbecome him; he looked quite Eastern, except that he is so fair . . . and when I put my large Cashmere about him, there was as fine a young bey, dey, or pacha improvised, as you would wish to see.[32]

Graham is, in this scene, infantilized and unmanned by being dressed by his mother in women's clothing (her own) without his knowledge. The magical transformation effected here by the shawl is that this act of feminizing simultaneously turns him into a "bey, dey, or pacha"—a man who is both far more powerful than Graham is in real life and a figure of fun, a mama's boy and a ruler intimately associated in the popular English imagination with despotism and the fantasy of the seraglio. What Joan Copjec has called "the well-documented fantasy of an erotic and despotic colonial cloth" is, like all fairy-tale magic, full of unguessed effects.[33]

If Western art historians' work on Kashmiri textiles does not always avoid certain aspects of the mythologizing that surrounds them in Victorian literature, it is invaluable in that it provides a vocabulary for describing something we think we know (a shawl made of cashmere) but possibly do not. First, their preferred term, *Kashmir,* by delimiting a place of manufacture and not a fabric, suggests that (1) what we know as "cashmere" is, or can be, many things, and (2) the combination of textile and technique that made the shawls unique was historically and geographically circumscribed and needs to be considered separately from several categories of shawls that are commonly identified as "cashmere." Briefly, Kashmir shawls are understood to be those woven on hand looms from one of several grades of hair from two or more species of Asian goat. An 1865 article in *Once a Week* magazine titled "Cashmere Shawls: Of What Are They Made?" raises this question in the context of what the writer perceives to be widely varying quality among the "cashmere" shawls in London shops, and opines that the difference may be accounted for not only by the use of various blends of wild and domestic goat hair and fleece but also by the introduction of fine winter down from wild sheep, wolves, dogs, and yaks (whether this conjecture has any basis in fact is impossible to determine; it is certainly unlikely that the Muslim weavers of Kashmir would knowingly have used dog fur in their creations).[34] The shawls were woven using a unique twill-tapestry method known as kanikar, considered likely to be Iranian rather than Indian in origin; they were probably first produced in the late fifteenth or early sixteenth century, and continued to be made in much the same manner until increased European demand in the late eighteenth and early nineteenth centuries provoked modifications in both patterns and manufacturing techniques among the Kashmiri makers. In addition, a vast range of machine-made European imitations were produced beginning in the first decade of the nineteenth century that may or may not have been sold as "véritable Cachemires."

The often-repeated truism available to Victorians was that Kashmir shawls were "immutable," "designed for Eternity in the unchanging East; copied from patterns which are the heirloom of a caste, and woven by fatalists, to be worn by adorers of the ancient garment, who resent the idea of the smallest change."[35] This claim, of course, directly contradicts the facts of the Kashmiri shawl industry. In taking issue with the classical economists on the relative autonomy of production and distribution from one another, Marx argued in the *Grundrisse* that distribution preceded production in crucial respects. Making his argument that distribution of the means of production, which necessarily shapes the character of what is then produced, must be considered, he uses a striking example.

> A conquering people divides the land among the conquerors, thus imposes a certain distribution and form of property in land, and thus determines production. Or it enslaves the conquered and so makes slave labour the foundation of production. Or a people rises in revolution and smashes the great landed estates into small parcels, and hence, by this new distribution, gives production a new character. . . . In all these cases, and they are all historical, it seems that distribution is not structured and determined by production, but rather the opposite, production by distribution.[36]

Writing in 1857–58, the time of the Rebellion and its bloody aftermath, it is perhaps not surprising that Marx is thinking about imperialism and revolution; after all, he wrote at least thirty-two articles on India in that two-year period. Although the case of Indian shawl manufacture proves his point nicely, his example leaves out the British modus operandi: the conquering power arrogates to itself the means of production and in so doing decimates the indigenous industry even as it depends upon a certain public perception of that industry to market its goods. An abundance of evidence regarding design, manufacture, and materials makes possible the mapping of the industry's attempts to adapt to the European market, and its eventual debilitation and downfall. The design element most closely associated with Kashmir shawls, which came to be known as "Paisley" after the city in which imitation shawls were manufactured, is a case in point. (In French, "cachemire" typically refers to the abstract-teardrop shape itself, so closely have the material and the paisley pattern been linked since the 1850s. Today, cashmere garments of French manufacture are often labeled with the English word "cashmere" rather than the French.)

In an article tracing the sources and evolution of the Paisley motif in Kashmir shawls, Rebecca Wells Corrie argues that floral ornamentation of textiles, which flourished in Northern India under the Mughals, became "increasingly stylized" throughout the eighteenth century, and that a stylized version of a popular "vase of flowers" design eventually mingled with a similarly common cypress motif to produce a single ornamental form, which tends to appear in neat rows on the borders of late eighteenth-century shawls.[37] Corrie disputes the thesis of earlier textile historians that this motif is a direct descendant of ancient lotus-bud and tree-of-life motifs that had earlier served as specific religious and royal symbols. Rather, it "carried some royal or sacred connotations," as suggested further by its resemblance to the mango-shaped royal symbol seen elsewhere in South Asia, but represented a revival, and not the persistence, of such forms and therefore cannot be said to carry the ancient meanings in as direct or uncomplicated a fashion as some have asserted.[38] Furthermore, Corrie cites evidence that by the early eighteenth century, designs apparently taken from English herbals, or illustrated books of plants and flowers, were appearing in Indian textiles worn by members of the Mughal court.[39] She writes, "Curiously, the shawl motif of the eighteenth and nineteenth centuries has roots spread so extensively through the ancient Near East and India that it has escaped clear definition as a step child [*sic*] of European colonialism," which in her estimation it

clearly is.[40] When the motif was brought to Europe to be copied, designers who were most likely unaware of the naturalistic roots of this already-
stylized form turned it into the elongated and almost purely abstract
shape—"paisley"—that adorned shawls from the 1850s on.

The conflation of the terms *cashmere* (which can refer to a place, a
fabric, a shawl, and in French, the paisley motif itself) and *paisley* (which
can refer to a place, a shawl, or a design element) serves to obscure the
history of the British centers of shawl production, Edinburgh, Norwich,
and Paisley. According to Pamela Clabburn, high-quality imitation Indian shawls were made in Edinburgh as early as 1793, but the majority of
high-end shawls were manufactured in Norwich, with twenty manufacturers in place by 1800.[41] Most firms used freelance designers who copied
widely from extant South Asian and French patterns. Paisley, on the
other hand, was known in the late eighteenth century as a center for the
production of muslin with a population of highly skilled weavers.[42] The
Paisley shawl industry emerged slightly after Norwich's and made many
types of shawls in addition to those of faux-Indian design, but was
known for mass-producing copies of finer Norwich "Kashmir" shawls, to
the consternation of Norwich manufacturers and their clients. But by
1818 the overseas market for such shawls had expanded from Turkey to
Persia to India, where they were sold as the "Paisley Kashmir."[43] Thus it
was the foreign trade that grafted the name of a Scottish city onto the
shawls and, eventually, the design element. Although there is a certain
logic to the abstracted "stepchild" motif's bearing a Western name, its Indian origins, which were obvious to the nineteenth-century observer, led
John Ruskin in 1859 to use shawl patterns as an example of art produced
by "cruel and savage nations, cruel in temper, savage in habits and conception" that produce art and design that exist purely to give pleasure
"without caring to convey any truth" about nature.[44] Thus the paisley
pattern, cut loose from its naturalistic moorings, returned to India both
as commodity and cultural condemnation.

John Irwin traces a more straightforward path from the floral motif to
the paisley than does Corrie, but he concurs that by the 1850s, "the Kashmir industry was largely under the domination of French merchants who
had settled there, bringing with them their own pattern-books for native
designers to copy."[45] Furthermore, the goat hair used in the shawls, besides varying widely in quality and fineness, was not necessarily a Kashmiri product but was purchased from sources in Ladakh and western Ti-

bet, and from Yarkant and Hotan (in present-day China), whose wool was apparently sold exclusively to the Kashmiris.[46] A final complication lies in the fact that some of the very finest shawls were not woven from domestic goat hair at all but from the fine winter undercoat of the wild ibex, which was in theory harvested from the shrubs on which the animal rubbed off its excess each spring. (Evidence suggests that in fact the animals were hunted for their valuable coats.) This wool was known as *shah tus* rather than *pashmina* (goat-hair fiber).[47]

The textile historians' work thus begins to chip away at the Kashmir shawl's mythical status by demonstrating that the shawls' existence was no more magical or amazing than that of any other highly realized art form but evolved within a complex network of cultural exchanges and trade opportunities. It also raises the possibility that by the mid-Victorian era, many "real cashmere" shawls were of questionable provenance. Thus, in *Vanity Fair,* the fact that Jos Sedley returns from Bengal with a "white Cashmere shawl" for his sister Amelia might have suggested to Victorian readers both that such a shawl would have been genuine and that Jos was cheap: plain white shawls were the most common and inexpensive of those manufactured in Kashmir but were therefore most likely to have been genuine, as imitations were generally patterned.[48] As Buie writes, "The earliest Kashmir shawls were often made of twill-woven *pashmina* [goat-hair fiber] with no decoration and were dyed or left a natural ivory. Plain shawls such as these, which were woven in Kashmir as a staple good since they could be produced quickly, persisted throughout the history of shawl manufacture."[49] Patterned shawls, which could take up to eighteen months to make, would have been far rarer in 1810 and were more likely to be worn by nobility than by members of the prosperous middle class.

Vanity Fair does not recount the precise means by which the shawls were obtained; as in most English novels, we only see them once they enter the realm of the domestic, where they are offered up to women as gifts.[50] Men play a peculiar role in the novelistic acquisition of shawls: they not only pay for them, they frequently procure them as well. The women's shopping trip to purchase dress fabric or bonnet trimming is a stock scene in English domestic novels, and the author of "Cashmere Shawls: Of What Are They Made?" claims ironically that "every lady who counts amongst her accomplishments the art of shopping, can with unerring precision select a shawl of real Cashmere manufacture out of a

promiscuous heap of others, whether of British or foreign manufacture."[51] Yet despite the appearance of several shawl vendors in London by
the 1830s,[52] shawls in novels are invariably gifts or commissions from
travelers to the East. Thus the shawl becomes a kind of ritual of casting-
off for the returning man—he restores himself to England and to Englishness by handing over to the women a garment that was commonly
understood to be worn in India by men.[53] In Elizabeth Gaskell's *Cranford,* Matty's mother is buried in the shawl sent from India by her son Peter, which arrives the day after her death; the buried shawl comes to stand
in for Peter himself, who is later believed dead by the family. (A
significant counterexample occurs in *Lady Audley's Secret;* preparing to be
"hustled suddenly away" after both her fraud and her ostensible madness
have been exposed, Lady Audley wraps herself in "an Indian shawl . . .
that had cost Sir Michael a hundred guineas."[54] The status markers of a
social-climbing impostor like Lucy Audley would naturally come from
the marketplace.) In her article "Shawls, Jewelry, Curry, and Rice in Victorian Britain," Nupur Chaudhuri writes that in order to "protect their
status as rulers and defend British culture in India, the Anglo-Indians
during the nineteenth century chose racial exclusiveness and altogether
rejected Indian goods and dishes" while residing in India.[55] She then
traces the manner in which Indian cultural artifacts were exploited for
cash or social status once their possessors were safely back in England:
women themselves frequently bought and sold shawls by placing and an-
swering ads in magazines. Such commerce is rarely depicted in fiction, although in Margaret Oliphant's 1883 novel *Hester,* which takes place in the
late 1860s, the widowed Mrs. John Vernon acquires the money to buy her
daughter ball gowns by "sacrific[ing]" her own Indian shawl, "which, after Hester and [her] pearls, was the thing in the world which the poor
lady held most dear."[56] For the most part, domestic novels prefer to de-
pict middle-class women giving gifts or donating to charity rather than
selling their belongings or buying previously owned clothing.[57] By be-
stowing Indian shawls upon their female relatives, then, men at once replaced themselves in domestic space and left open the amusing possibility of playing at being "Oriental." Safely at home in Europe, the middle
class is free to flaunt Indian servants, eat curry, decorate the home with
Indian knickknacks, and generally to act out in a properly circumscribed
fashion the nightmare fantasy of "going native."

Perhaps the most bizarre instance of Kashmir shawl as plot device occurs in an utterly forgotten 1840 novel by Charles White, titled *The Cashmere Shawl: An Eastern Fiction*. The novel's introduction is a frame narrative in which a London writer discovers that a new packet of stationery that has just been delivered to his home ("a quire of that delicate, hot pressed, coloured paper, adorned with an embossed tracery of cupids and flowers, which peradventure one may sometimes have occasion to employ for tender purposes") is trying to communicate with him—in Persian.[58] The writer, alarmed, replies, "are you a dive [an evil spirit in Persian mythology] or jin? Speak!"[59] Strikingly, the English writer/narrator immediately understands that he is in the realm of the Oriental supernatural. After ascertaining that the talking piece of paper is not a devil, and making it "swear to behave discreetly" the writer agrees to release it from the packet in which it is being smothered.[60] The talking paper replies, "I swear by the beard of Ali, on whom be the peace and benediction of Allah, that I will obey you in everything. . . . If you are not satisfied with that oath, I will swear by the day break and ten nights [a reference to the opening of the eighty-ninth chapter of the Koran]—by that which is double, and that which is single;—in short, by the whole Koran."[61] Apparently, then, this piece of paper is not only a Muslim but specifically a Shi'ite, as were the Kashmiri Muslims for whom shawl weaving was a hereditary occupation.

Commanded by the writer to tell its story, the piece of paper begins.

Well then! I was once a splendid Cashmere shawl . . . Yes! I was formerly one of the most costly shawls that ever issued from the looms of Islamabad. I have witnessed many singular adventures, both in the east and west. I have been the envied inhabitant of harems, palaces and bagnios. I have shaded the brows of Sultans, Pachas, Omrahs and Khans. I have girded the waists of Sultanas, Princesses, Khanums and Bayaderes. I have passed through many hands; enjoyed great glories, and alas—devoured infinite dirt. Until at length—O destiny! When worn out, soiled, tattered and thread bare as a half naked dervish, I was sold to a rag merchant. From his impure clutches, I found my way into the boiler of a paper manufacturer, and thence *Ey vah*! behold what I am now! But Allah is great and merciful. His power knows no limits. He has loosened the knot of my tongue, and I still retain some remnant of my former beauty, with the sense and memory of an animate and rational being.[62]

The narrator concludes his story by informing the reader that he has rendered the shawl's narrative "to the best of my power, into English, and divested of much of its Oriental idioms, and flowery phraseology;—a task rendered the more difficult since, as the learned reader will easily perceive, the story was narrated in a mixture of Persian, Turkish, Arabic, and other eastern dialects."[63] He concludes, "if the critical reader should consider that too much of this phraseology still remains in my version, he must attribute it to my desire that the narrative should strictly retain its Oriental character, and be answerable to its title of 'a Romance of the East.'"[64] What follows, in the shawl's first-person narration, is three volumes of what by 1840 were fairly predictable Oriental tales, beginning with the shawl's life as a goat and its subsequent transformation into a garment. The suggestive device of a blank sheet of paper with a story to tell is shortly overshadowed by stories of war, seduction, and intrigue, but the shawl's garrulous insistence on its centrality to the events occurring around it and its rightful place in the Eastern courts in which it finds itself, its Muslim identity, and its place on the bodies of male and female royalty are jarringly at odds with Kashmir shawls' burgeoning reputation as a status marker of bourgeois Englishwomen. Despite the public's fascination with Kashmir shawls, White's collection of tales seems to have sunk without a trace; unlike his other novels, it was printed in only one edition. He has mythologized the shawl, but in precisely the wrong way: his talking shawl is decidedly, even aggressively, foreign, and thus its only connection to the English is first as an observer of their incursions into foreign lands and then as a foreigner itself in England.

The more mainstream midcentury novels consistently remove Kashmir shawls not only from the cash nexus, or the realm of commodification, but from their place of origin as well. They do so not only by making the shawls gifts the purchase of which we never witness, but by portraying shawls either as old but stately garments that women seem always to have owned or else explicitly as heirlooms that women inherit rather than purchase. In Elizabeth Gaskell's *North and South,* a novel in which textiles circulate continually, Indian shawls are largely stripped of their foreign (or at least Asian) resonances and instead stand in for the established (as opposed to the new and vulgar), the handmade (as opposed to factory-woven Manchester calico), and that which can only be inherited or handed down, never purchased. As the novel opens, the wealthy widow Mrs. Shaw is preparing to give her collection of "Indian shawls and scarfs,"[65] which she received as gifts from her late husband, to her soon-to-be-married daughter Edith. Edith, however, a small "soft ball of muslin and ribbon, and silken curls,"[66] is "half-smothered" in the imposing garments and uses them instead as picnic rugs; it is her tall, "queenly" cousin Margaret on whom this "garb of a princess" finds its appropriate model.[67] As Annette B. Weiner and Jane Schneider write in their introduction to *Cloth and Human Experience,*

> Capitalist production and its associated cultural values reordered the symbolic potential of cloth . . . [by] altering the process of manufacture, capitalism eliminated the opportunity for weavers and dyers to infuse their product with spiritual value and to reflect and pronounce on analogies between reproduction and production.[68]

Certainly, social reproduction is at stake in the handing down of prized textiles from mother to daughter.[69] Much anxiety is expended over the fact that Margaret ought to but does not have the kind of patrimony that makes Edith so desirable a match.

Margaret's own Indian shawl, which she wears "as an empress wears her drapery," seems to have much to do with the discomfort she provokes in the calico manufacturer Mr. Thornton at their first meeting.[70] Margaret's identification with handcrafted rather than mass-produced goods is furthered by her well-bred horror at the "atrocious" wallpaper in the Hales' new home in Crampton, which Mr. Thornton orders redone because after meeting Margaret, he is "ashamed of having imagined that [the house] would do very well for the Hales, in spite of a certain vulgarity in it which had struck him at the time of his looking it over."[71] The effect of "vulgarity" is largely produced by the wallpaper, which had begun to be mass-produced only in 1841;[72] Gaskell's implication is that in their slower-moving and more refined southern town, Hales were accustomed to hand-printed wallpaper. Yet despite the bad taste the Thorntons display in their garish home, they are not exactly beneath the Hales in the novel's code of textiles; Mrs. Thornton impresses Mrs. Hale at their first meeting by wearing lace "of that old English point which has not been made for this seventy years, and which cannot be bought."[73]

Thus *North and South* wants to value a past in which India's and England's textile industries are on equal terms as producers of first-quality handmade objects, but finally, in the resolution of its marriage plot (in which Margaret both inherits land and marries Mr. Thornton), it sides with Manchester. In so doing, it unites north and south, land-based and manufacturing wealth, the Establishment and the worthy newcomer[74] while gesturing obliquely at the union occurring just outside the picture: in the nineteenth century, the two-hundred-year-old tension was eased somewhat between the traders who made vast profits importing desirable Indian textiles and the English textile trade, which resented the competition. The industrial novels tell and retell the story of English handloom weavers who were left to starve as the Industrial Revolution made their trade obsolete; what remains largely unarticulated is the fact that England's domestic economy could not have absorbed the increasing amounts of factory-made cotton cloth produced in England. Rather, the cotton manufacturers united to sell cotton cloth in South Asia, aided by the colonial government and the British army, who systematically dismantled India's textile industries in order to create a market for these new imported goods. In a colonial version of tommy-shops, company stores from which miners were forced to buy shoddy goods at inflated prices, administrators in India turned a profit by forcing the native populations to purchase British-made textiles.[75] Although even the passive Edith notices that the (presumably French) calico in Corfu is less expensive and of better quality than that which she habitually purchased in England, Margaret's evolution into a mill owner's wife serves to valorize Manchester and an industry whose remarkable expansion, commonly attributed to advances in machine technology, was in reality driven by the increase in markets brought about by the expansion of the empire.

That shawls in *North and South* are usually referred to as "Indian" rather than "cashmere" points to another potential source of confusion about their origins, especially those purchased abroad by East India Company employees: there may have been good reason for sellers of Indian shawls to conflate "Indian" and "Cashmere," knowing as they did that the middle-class English market did not necessarily understand the difference between the shawls produced in Kashmir and high-quality shawls from other regions of India. To speak of Kashmir as part of the East India Company's territories, as it is commonly assumed to have been, however, would be inaccurate. By the mid-nineteenth century, the distinctions between "British India" and the territories proper were slippery at best;[76] nevertheless, Kashmir in 1846 had the unenviable distinction of being sold by the British to a Sikh ally, Ghulab Singh, even though it had never been formally under British control. The first Anglo-

Sikh war, which lasted only from December 1845 to March 1846 and consisted of four major campaigns, had nevertheless cost over a thousand British lives, far more than the public was accustomed to expect in colonial actions, and thus brought more attention to the Punjab and Kashmir than ever before. From that point forward, "News from the Punjab" was a familiar if unwelcome heading in the *Times* of London. In addition to disposing of Kashmir and giving the British widespread powers in the Punjab (which was formally annexed in 1849 at the close of the second Sikh War), the Treaty of Amritsar, signed at the first war's conclusion, required that Kashmir's new ruler, Ghulab Singh, acknowledge "the supremacy of the British Government and . . . in token of supremacy present annually to the British Gov't, one horse, twelve perfect shawl goats of approved breed (six male and six female), and three pairs of Kashmiri shawls."[77] These shawls were sent each year to Queen Victoria and shifted back toward being what *Household Words* had imagined them to be in 1852: royal tributes. (In "Shawls," Martineau writes, "For thousands of years have Eastern potentates made presents of shawls to distinguished strangers.")[78] Victoria herself, even before being named Empress of India in 1876, took up the ritual of giving Indian shawls as gifts to visiting dignitaries. Describing this practice, Adrienne Munich notes that Victoria in many such ways "imported India to England. . . . For her, as for many subjects, India gave Britain a symbol of empire."[79]

But as Irwin points out, although the Norwich and Paisley shawl industries had been producing imitation machine-made Kashmir shawls since the turn of the century, by the 1860s they were ubiquitous. In England,

> by 1870 a Jacquard-woven Paisley shawl could be bought for as little as [one pound], and the identical pattern printed on cotton for only a few shillings. Thus, the Kashmir style, originally a mark of exclusiveness and exotic rarity, had now become vulgar and mundane as a result of its popularity.[80]

"Cashmere Shawls: Of What Are They Made?" asserts that the London shawl market had been in a downturn since 1860.[81] As Ruskin's comments on Indian savagery suggest, the rebellion of 1857 known as the Mutiny and particularly the way it was presented to the English reading public,[82] while not entirely accountable for this downturn, nevertheless produced a wave of anti-Indian sentiment that temporarily cooled the popular taste for Indian commodities. Ruskin spells out for us the underside of Orientalism: romanticizing Kashmir shawls may turn into demonizing within the same conceptual framework.

Yet Orientalist aesthetics, as Edward Said argues, are inextricable from politics and economics, and political and economic developments influenced the shift in fashion that, on the surface at least, brought the shawl market to the point of collapse. The Franco-Prussian War damaged the French market for Kashmiri goods, and the influx of imitations simultaneously diminished the status of Kashmir shawls and priced them out of the market in both England and Western Europe. The Kashmir shawl industry was abandoned by European traders, and many of the shawl makers, faced with starvation in the Kashmir famine of 1877–79, emigrated to the Punjab.[83] In 1901, an article in the *Magazine of Art* through its title pronounced Kashmir shawl making to be "An Extinct Art"; although the article names "the Franco-German War" and "the abolition of forced labour in Kashmir" as the primary causes, this opinion, while generally accepted in the West, is frequently disputed by Indian historians.[84] N. N. Raina, for example, argues that the collapse by 1880 of an industry that in 1865 had employed 30,000 workers was due primarily to the influx of cheap British shawls in European markets; the British claim that the Franco-Prussian War was to blame is, he asserts, an "alibi."[85]

Thus the precarious balance between Englishness and exoticism was tipped by a cascade of events that served at once to focus public attention on the Indian shawls' place of origin and to muddy their identity through widespread imitation. Women's bodies were still the site of elaborate systems of class demarcation, but the signs themselves shifted, and this shift was recorded in one of the few novels of the 1880s that mentioned shawls at all. Readers of *Hester,* who would recognize a time roughly fifteen years before by the outworn fashions Oliphant carefully evokes—Ellen's *thés dansantes* and Hester's tarlatan ball gowns[86]—would also see the wisdom of Mrs. John's decision, when forced to part with one of the two prized possessions of her own youth in the 1840s, to sell her Indian shawl and keep her pearls for her daughter to wear. Although she is attached to the shawl, it can no longer do the crucial work of marking Hester as a young woman of distinction, while the pearls still perform flawlessly.

By the end of the nineteenth century, older and finer specimens of twill-tapestry weaving were being collected by museums, but the shawls themselves were utterly devalued as fashion. When the worldly and self-absorbed Mrs. Allonby in Oscar Wilde's 1894 play *A Woman of No Importance* directs young Gerald Arbuthnot to bring her "something nice from your travels" (having failed to absorb the fact that Gerald has rejected the idea of being an imperial adventurer and is staying home), this consummate woman of fashion cautions, "not an Indian shawl—on no account an Indian shawl."[87]

CHAPTER TWO

Mechanization, Free Trade, and Imperialism: Cotton

In *Manchester Men and Indian Cotton,* Arthur Silver writes that

> until the Revolutionary Wars at the end of the eighteenth century India
> had been a source of luxury goods for British home consumption and for
> her foreign trade. In the course of the late eighteenth and early nine-
> teenth centuries there was a complete reversal of this relationship. From
> a source of trade goods India became a market for Britain's manufactures
> and a source of raw materials for her expanding industries.[1]

Although this statement may be qualified with regard to a few select
commodities such as tea, it certainly obtains in the case of cotton. Cotton textiles were relatively scarce in England prior to the seventeenth century, when the textile trade with India gained momentum; the unprecedented popularity of Indian cloth gave rise to widely voiced concerns
about its effect on such disparate subjects as servants' morality and the
British wool trade. English manufacturers' desire to usurp the market of
so lucrative a commodity led to bans on Indian cotton goods (although
several of these were short-lived) and eventually to their widespread domestic imitation; in the mid-nineteenth century, the Manchester cotton
manufacturers attempted to ameliorate their dependence upon the U.S.
cotton supply by promoting cotton cultivation in India.[2] The history of
this long and contentious relationship is woven into both domestic and
industrial novels through repeated references to Indian cotton. Yet while
domestic novels tend to mention cotton textiles primarily in terms of the
private and the personal, particularly as women's dress (which in turn is

understood to speak to their character and social class), industrial novels are also concerned with cotton as commodity. In both instances, however, cotton's foreign origins are often gestured at, but never quite emerge from the background to become part of the narrative. In other words, cotton emerges as text despite relentless efforts to reduce it to context.

Indian cotton textiles were crucial to the early mercantile successes of the East India Company. In *The Honourable Company,* John Keay writes that the *Merchant's Hope,* which sailed from Surat to England in 1613 with a cargo of cotton goods, marked the beginning of a new domestic economy.

> Instead of English tweeds revolutionizing Eastern fashions, Indian cottons were about to invade English domestic life. Napkins and table-cloths, bed sheets and soft furnishings, not to mention underwear and dress fabrics, quite suddenly became indispensable to every respectable household. A new vocabulary of chintzes and calicoes, taffetas, muslins, ginghams and cashmeres entered everyday use. Having first invaded the larder, Eastern produce was about to take over the linen cupboard.[3]

Here, the room-by-room takeover of the English home by Indian textiles at once prefigures and justifies the British movement into India. More striking, however, is the way that the textiles' gradual movement into the beds and onto the bodies of the English is figured as an "invasion," whereas the failed movement of tweeds into South Asia would have "revolutionized" India. These loaded and opposing figures of revolution and invasion might more be apposite if we reversed them. "Invasion" suggests force, intrusion, infestation; to revolutionize is to change radically. The advent of Indian cotton textiles in England did revolutionize it in the sense that customs and social meanings underwent significant shifts as a result; the nineteenth-century movement of British cotton goods into India was an invasion in the sense that an already-existing industry was targeted, attacked, and weakened. At the same time, however, the "vocabulary of chintzes and calicoes" made its way into Victorian novels as a means of signaling stability, continuity, and order.

Indian cotton textiles became widely popular during the seventeenth century, but their importation into England was checked if by no means ended by 1701. Beginning in this year, protectionist legislation restricted the import of many categories of textiles into England except those destined to be reexported. The fact that the English controlled, and thus profited by, much of the textile trade in Bengal in the eighteenth century, however, meant that the flow of Indian textiles into England continued.[4] The juggling of cargoes ostensibly meant to be resold abroad, as well as outright smuggling, kept a constellation of desirable fabrics within reach of the English public despite official bans. As Silver makes clear, English textile manufacturers were from the outset at the forefront of efforts to keep Indian cloth out of England, thus placing them at odds with the merchants who stood to make vast profits from the trade. The manufacturers were initially unsuccessful; in 1664 alone over 250,000 pieces of calico were imported into England, a number that represented 73 percent of the Company's imports for that year.[5] At first the English used Indian cotton largely to make accessories: aprons, petticoats, headdresses, hoods, sleeves, nightgowns, pockets, cravats, cuffs, handkerchiefs, and shirts, in addition to bedclothes and curtains, were crafted from Indian calico, chintz, and muslin.[6] But as larger, more visible garments such as women's dresses began to be made of these fabrics, and as demand increased, a backlash gathered force. Beverly Lemire writes,

> The establishment of . . . new decencies among the middling orders and the fostering of new wants among the labouring people threatened accepted views and precipitated a crisis. . . . [Detractors argued that] the popularity of calicoes among almost all ranks of the people blurred the boundaries in the social hierarchy to an intolerable degree, to the detriment of the health, order, and prosperity of the kingdom.[7]

The backlash, then, was not an abandonment by consumers, as was the case with the Kashmir shawls I discuss in chapter 1. Rather, it was a reaction to the very popularity of the textiles, a popularity that was understood to have pernicious political and economic effects. Ann Rosalind Jones and Peter Stallybrass have noted that in the early modern period, "the [idea] that foreign fashions dismember the body politic was a commonplace," although it may be argued that the moral panic over cotton textiles was primarily a displacement of economic fears.[8] Furthermore, the introduction of Indian cotton to England threatened to disorder the elaborate codes of signification and articulation surrounding dress that Jones and Stallybrass identify and analyze. The circulation of used clothing that structured and reinforced hierarchical social relationships would be upended by an economy that allowed servants and other household dependents to purchase or make new clothes of their own choosing. In the late seventeenth century, however, this social threat was frequently voiced in terms of an economic argument: imported cotton would, it was widely believed, ruin the domestic wool and silk trades. Although this was untrue to the degree that cotton goods were creating new categories of dress rather than usurping old ones, the wool trade did suffer to some extent. Wool manufacturers mounted a campaign against cotton; Lemire explains, "The barrage of abuse [directed against Indian textiles] grew in proportion to the popularity of the Indian fabrics in the home market."[9] Wool producers lobbied Parliament, whose first move to defend the industry was a 1678 law requiring that the dead be buried wrapped in English wool; lawmakers were, however, unsuccessful in passing several attempts to force similar requirements upon the living.[10] Parliament and the wool traders thereafter shifted their tactics and began to focus on eliminating the competition from imported cotton textiles. A bill to ban the importation of "painted, dyed, printed or stained" Indian textiles, introduced but defeated in 1696 and 1697, was passed in 1701 (plain unfinished and white materials were still legal).[11] Crude domestic imitations of chintz and calico began gradually to appear, and although they too were condemned by the defenders of English wool, they were popular in a market in which cotton clothing was now firmly established. In 1721, Parliament banned virtually all imported cotton textiles, and the domestic cotton industry began its ascendancy.

A profound shift in the vexed relationship between the East India Company traders and the English textile manufacturers occurred as the race in the second half of the eighteenth century to imitate domestically the colors, textures, and patterns of Indian cloth gave rise to a series of technological innovations that we have retrospectively named the Industrial Revolution. These innovations made it possible to produce far more fabric than the domestic market could absorb; English cotton manufacturers began early in the nineteenth century to seek foreign and especially imperial markets for their surpluses. But first, the textile manufacturers flooded domestic markets with inexpensive goods, sharply curtailing the market for the now more costly but still available Indian textiles.

Yet even as the English market underwent such a shift, and as Indian textile industries crumbled under British pressure on Indian consumers to purchase English-made goods and the withdrawal of British investment,[12] Indian textiles are mythologized in domestic novels as the most desirable, the standard against which other cloth is judged. Details of dress are critical to the cultural work that Victorian novels attempt to do; in marking fine distinctions of social status and individual taste, they communicate what might be termed an ethics of style. In an era in which brand-names barely existed, in a novelistic universe in which women (and, frequently, men) did not choose professions, the choices or necessities of dress were understood to speak not only to a character's individual taste or income level but to her intelligence, her habits of mind, her morality.[13] This was true for women in particular because, as an anonymous 1865 article by Anne Mozley in *Blackwood's* titled "Dress" suggests,[14]

> With the young dress is almost the only thing they can call their own; with the great majority of women it includes all to which they can ever in strict truth apply the potent, influential, entrancing words "my" and "mine." A wife is indeed permitted by custom to say "my house;" "my drawing room," and her cook can say "my kitchen;" but in these cases a third party has the stronger ownership. The moral effects of independent possession depend on its strict reality; and with most women their dress is their one tenement and holding—the one thing that, once theirs, is acknowledged theirs by law and custom.[15]

In this argument, not only is the possession of private property presumed to produce salutary moral effects, but the ownership of clothing extends metaphorically to moral ownership of one's person, which has the effect of proper self-regulation (Mozley continues, "All slatternliness or meanness of attire marks some intellectual deficiency").[16] The outer reality is thus a faithful reproduction of the inner, or in theological terms, the woman's properties are communicated through her accidents. The argument for clothing as self-ownership frequently appears, if implicitly, in novelistic descriptions of women's and girls' clothing. For example, Suzanne Keen has argued that the "Quakerish" dresses favored by Dorothea Brooke and Jane Eyre, which paradoxically "emphasiz[e] . . . the female body as an object of the male gaze," signify not always or only sexlessness or plainness but also "marriageability and the promise of sexual fulfillment; respectability . . . reforming tendencies; social consciousness; and a body that may be moved by the spirit to speak."[17] The appropriately clothed body thus shapes the social values around it by reflecting an unimpeachable inner reality. This is, of course, wishful thinking; novelists may use spotless Dacca muslin in particular as a sign of female virtue, but women's clothing in general is often accorded more suspicion as that which hides rather than reveals what's beneath.

Elizabeth Gaskell's novels are obsessively preoccupied with details of dress and furnishings as they relate to gendered social norms and moral codes. Yet because Gaskell insists on using places of origin to demonstrate her characters' command of taste, her apparent domestication of textiles somehow refuses to stay at home. Furthermore, the repetitive nature of her descriptions, her insistent circling back to reiterations of similar details, creates the sense that the reader is being schooled, that what is clamorously taken for granted in the novel might in fact be underacknowledged in the world that the text purports to represent faithfully. Gaskell's prose thus subtly foregrounds the fact of Indian trade while ignoring its relevance to much of anything outside the construction of properly circumscribed middle-class female subjectivity. *Wives and Daughters* begins by linking the familial, the social, and the sartorial as formative influences; the novel opens with a vast perspective that moves ever closer until it alights upon its heroine, Molly Gibson, in bed—"To begin with the old rigmarole of childhood. In a country there was a shire, and in that shire was a town, and in that town there was a house, and in that house there was a room, and in that room there was a bed, and in that bed there lay a little girl" who the day before has lined the bonnet that she is to wear to a garden party.[18] Although the nursery-rhyme structure playfully suggests that this story about a child is perhaps nothing more than a children's story, the telescoping of England into Molly's bed has deeper implications for the novel's relationship to the home and the world. The moral influence of the environment that Molly shapes and is shaped by is identified with the larger society in which she moves, with her immediate physical surroundings, in this case a "little white dimity bed," and with the clothes she wears.[19] Molly's identity, national, local, and familial, and the interconnectedness of the spheres in which she will move are thus foregrounded even as she is introduced as the unique being on whom the narrative will focus.

As Franco Moretti has observed, the nineteenth-century bildungsroman offers "one of the most harmonious solutions . . . to a dilemma coterminous with modern bourgeois civilization: the conflict between the ideal of *self-determination* and the equally imperious demands of *socialization*."[20] Molly's narrative of socialization, coded as one of moral

development, is worked out in terms of "taste," and specifically the textiles and decorative objects that she sews, wears, and learns to admire,
many of which are explicitly described as being of Indian origin. The
novel opens on the morning Molly is to pay her first annual visit, with
the other villagers, to The Towers, home of Lord and Lady Cumnor, the
great personages of her country town toward whom "a very pretty
amount of feudal feeling still lingered."[21] Molly has prepared for this
great occasion by taking "infinite pains" to plait "a neat little quilling,"
with a blue bow attached, to line her bonnet.[22] *Plait* in this context
means "pleat" rather than "braid"; to *quill* fabric is to press or sew small
ridges into it. This type of sewing, at once painstaking, ornamental, and
practical, mediates between the positive and negative qualities associated
with needlework. It requires mental and physical discipline and a mod-
icum of skill, and furthers an ideal of what Jones and Stallybrass call
"obedient domesticity."[23] At the same time, this "very first bit of such
finery Molly had ever had the prospect of wearing," as Gaskell drolly
names it, is inside the bonnet; its chief admirer is Molly herself.[24] Like
lace-trimmed underskirts, quilling is in one sense an acceptable form of
feminine adornment because it barely shows itself to the world; on the
other hand, decorating the hidden parts of one's clothing for personal
pleasure veers toward an inappropriate level of frivolity and self-involve-
ment (or simply a waste of time). Yet the very interiority of the quilling
suggests that the virtuous response to achievement is private satisfaction,
not public triumph; display should be always beside the point. Interior
beauty is durable; describing the "heavy and serviceable" cotton hand-
kerchief that covers Molly's "solid" straw bonnet, Gaskell writes, in an
aside typical of the narrator's commentary, "if the [bonnet] underneath it
had been a flimsy fabric of gauze and lace and flowers, it would have been
altogether [crushed]."[25]

Pitting the child-character against her hyperfeminine, social-climbing rival, Gaskell reveals that at the garden party, Molly feels her first
glimmers of distrust toward Mrs. Kirkpatrick, her future stepmother,
who is effortlessly gracious in the presence of the nobility and frequently
unkind otherwise, and who disparages the heaviness of Molly's bonnet,
thus turning what the narrator extols as its chief virtue into a fault.[26]
Later in the novel Mrs. Kirkpatrick, in putting together a trousseau,
places display over propriety, in keeping with her "superficial and flimsy
character."[27]

What new articles she bought for herself, were such as would make a show, and an impression upon the ladies of Hollingford. She argued with herself that linen, and all underclothing, would never be seen; while she knew that every gown she had, would give rise to much discussion, and would be counted up in the little town.

So her stock of underclothing was very small, and scarcely any of it new; but it was made of dainty material, and was finely mended up by her deft fingers, many a night long after her pupils were in bed; inwardly resolving all the time she sewed, that hereafter someone else should do her plain-work.[28]

Mrs. Kirkpatrick's "genius for millinery and dress," which her daughter Cynthia shares, is thus of ambiguous value; it is a feminine virtue taken too far and like all extremes in Gaskell's universe is problematic.[29] By allowing its possessors to appear better than they are, it functions as a form of deceit. The many instances in which Gaskell reveals Mrs. Kirkpatrick's little deceptions and fabrications are thus the equivalent of showing us her underwear; all speak to that which her clothing hides. She has amassed enough experience from working for the wealthy to know what public gesture to make, but such proper action never emerges from her innate qualities. Unobserved, she inevitably betrays moral coarseness, and the lack of value she ascribes to those parts of her dress that remain hidden mirrors her lack of interest in the unobserved aspects of her married life.

Tropes of sewing and clothing are further linked with household furnishings; throughout the course of the novel, Gaskell moves Molly among several houses including her own home, the home of her father's acquaintance Squire Hamley, to whom she pays an extended visit, and the homes of Lord Cumnor, which she visits briefly at the ages of twelve and seventeen. Her position as a doctor's daughter allows her to absorb critical information from visiting her social betters, but she is strongly influenced by the homes themselves, whose furnishings impact her notions of propriety in terms of dress, decor, and manners.

Gaskell repeatedly gives her main character lessons in good taste; early in the novel, Mrs. Hamley saves Molly from the humiliation of wearing plaid silk by recommending white muslin instead. Molly's ability to correct her error in judgment is due in part to the edifying influence of the Hamleys' tasteful and spotless home, particularly Molly's own "old-fashioned" room in which the "chintz curtains were Indian calico of the last century—the colours almost washed out, but the stuff itself exquisitely clean."[30] The description continues:

> The wooden flooring . . . was of finely-grained oak, so firmly joined, plank to plank, that no grain of dust could make its way into the interstices. There were none of the luxuries of modern days; no writing-table, or sofa, or pier-glass. In one corner of the walls was a bracket, holding an Indian jar filled with pot-pourri.[31]

The novel documents both the Hamleys' education of Molly and Molly's education of them: she learns to make moral as well as aesthetic distinctions about quality as she learns to prefer Roger to Osborne Hamley, and she eventually teaches Squire Hamley that she is not an ambitious intruder attempting to gain a foothold in the family but is worthy of being Roger's wife. When Molly goes to see her father married at one of Lord Cumnor's homes, she admires its resemblance to Hamley: "yellow satin upholstery of seventy or a hundred years ago, all delicately kept and scrupulously clean; great Indian cabinets, and china jars, emitting spicy odours."[32] To judge correctly, to see properly, involves interpreting tangibles as well as intangibles, and what Molly learns from upholstery she applies to her person. By the time her father marries, she knows enough to feel oppressed not only by her socially ambitious stepmother's "perpetual fidgetiness after details of ceremony and correctness of attendance"[33] but also the "various little tables, loaded with *objets d'art* (as Mrs Gibson delighted to call them)" that now fill her father's drawing-room.[34] For Gaskell, her heroine's taste in clothing and furniture, marked in part by a preference for Indian things in an English setting, is given more weight than her taste in books, music, or art.

Mrs. Kirkpatrick's "silkiness"[35] and ability to produce a smooth surface are opposed to Molly's own appearance; Gaskell describes Molly at age twelve and again at age seventeen as "wild."[36] But Molly is, briefly, transformed through the agency of Mrs. Kirkpatrick; she attends her father's wedding in a "fine India muslin"[37] which is "both so simple and so elegant as at once to charm Molly" and cause her to wonder "if I'm pretty. . . . I almost think I am."[38] Molly's ambivalence in this situation is the mark of her character; she is not just unsure that she's pretty, but unsure whether she ought even to be considering the question. Her moment of self-admiration is self-reflexive; unlike Mrs. Kirkpatrick, she can appreciate the surface quality of her dress without being herself only surface. It has long been observed that Victorian novels tend to value the interior and the personal over the structural in their anatomies of and solutions to social disorder. What is striking here, however, is that a foreign product functions prominently as the visible sign of Molly's English virtue and (eventual) correct aesthetic judgment, when as late as the mid-eighteenth century, Indian cotton fashions were seen as a threat to morality as well as to the economy. Once the threat is neutralized, however, Indian cotton cloth shifts from commodity to mythology.

White muslin dresses, freighted with associations of virtue and good taste, are virtually the uniform of young unmarried women in mid-Victorian novels. In Margaret Oliphant's *Miss Marjoribanks,* Lucilla Marjoribanks takes pride in having brought into fashion in Carlingford the "white [muslin] frock, high in the neck"[39] in which she regularly appears at her Thursday evening parties and which Elisabeth Jay argues conveys "a series of messages": "it demarcated the eligible virginal '*entourage* of white-robed angels' from the married women, privileged fine fabric and elegant cut, and emphasized the extreme respectability of evenings at which day bodices, covering the chest up to the neck, rather than the increasingly indecorous, low-cut evening gowns of the period, were to be worn."[40] At the same time, Oliphant's white muslin reveals "how chastity and gentility, those values most deeply embedded in the Victorian ideology of 'the feminine,' were manufactured and managed by a manipulation of signs."[41] This is undoubtedly true as regards muslin; to cite but one example, the more morally questionable young women in both Gaskell and Oliphant wear tired muslin dresses that have "seen one or two garden-parties" and "are not in the freshest order"[42] or are "six times washed [and] different from the spotless lightness of the draperies [of the other women]."[43] Signs in this case, however, are not without referents, however radically unmoored from them they may appear to be, and muslin in the nineteenth-century novel cannot be taken solely on its own terms as referring to English virgins, particularly given the frequency with which *muslin* is explicitly modified by the word *Indian*. The means by which a foreign textile demonized in 1696 as the moral and economic ruination of England came to carry the freight of "the Victorian feminine" by the mid-nineteenth century needs further exploration. It is only after the English body and the English nation can be satisfactorily thought to have been stripped of Indian textiles that they are permitted to make an attenuated return (the period of their lives during which women wore white muslin was relatively brief). Furthermore, Lucilla Marjoribanks's determination to put the young women of Carlingford into uniform, like her ambition to take upon herself the task of "knitting people together, and making a harmonious whole out of the scraps and fragments of society,"[44] speaks both to her outsize ambitions and her realization that such ambitions may only be realized within a feminized and circumscribed sphere. Joseph A. O'Mealy has noted the prevalence in *Miss Marjoribanks* of "mock heroic language, laced with imperial and military tropes";[45] he writes, "since [Lucilla] cannot partake in the imperial public life open to young men like her cousin Tom, who goes to India, she will create her own private empire in Carlingford"[46] in which she can realize her "vision of a parish saved, a village reformed, a county reorganized."[47] The virtue bodied forth by Lucilla's muslin is as much a public reforming virtue as a private one. Muslin suggests a paradoxical ability to move into the world without being marked by it, because muslin can be counted on to register the trace of the world at the slightest touch; it carries the ability to retain the spotlessness of the home in a dirty world, but only to the degree that it reflects the qualities of the wearer.

Unlike Keen's examples of Dorothea Brooke and Jane Eyre, whose dress reflects their moral core in a fairly unambiguous manner, Gaskell is somewhat more likely to weave a more complex text from her characters' dress.[48] In her second novel, *Ruth*, the eponymous heroine goes from being seen, when she first meets her seducer Henry Bellingham, in a "worn and shabby"[49] black silk dress, to appearing in Wales with Bellingham a few months later wearing, somewhat incongruously, a white gown purchased for her in London by Bellingham that gives her a "very modest and innocent-looking appearance."[50] The irony, of course, lies in the fact that Gaskell insists that Ruth *is* modest and innocent; she is living openly with a man to whom she is not married, yet is utterly unaware of the significance of this arrangement. When in London (a part of the story that Gaskell does not narrate but only refers to), Ruth, in her naïveté, chooses virginal white clothing "in preference to more expensive articles of dress when Mr. Bellingham had given her *carte blanche*."[51] She does not think of herself as a fallen or ruined woman and so fails to dress herself accordingly. Only when a small boy slaps her for admiring his baby sister and calls her a "bad, naughty girl"[52] does Ruth realize the truth of her situation. After Bellingham deserts her and Ruth learns that she is pregnant, her rescuers, the Bensons, convince her to pass herself off as a widow, and she returns to wearing black dresses, this time made of the "coarsest" and "homeliest" cloth available. She cuts up Bellingham's old gifts, the clothing made of "fine linen and delicate soft white muslin," and turns them into baby clothes "for the little creature, for whom in its white purity of soul nothing could be too precious."[53]

In the writing of *Ruth,* Gaskell walks a tricky moral line by at once insisting on her heroine's ignorance—when she meets Bellingham, she is a fifteen-year-old orphan, "innocent and snow-pure,"[54] who "was too young when her mother died to have received any cautions or words of advice respecting *the* subject of a woman's life"[55]—and her coming to consciousness of what is depicted as her great sin, one that in the novel's terms requires not only a lifetime of atonement but ultimately her life itself. At the same time, Gaskell insists that Ruth's son Leonard has no share in his parents' misdeeds and that public rejection of children born out of wedlock is itself sinful. Ruth's rending of her own garments and refashioning them as clothes for her unborn child even as she dresses herself in mourning marks at once her acknowledgment and renunciation of her sin and her insistence on her child's innocence while at the same time linking them both to the absent father for whom she truly (if secretly) mourns. The tearing apart and cutting up of the clothing Bellingham purchased for her suggests both an act of grief and a gesture symbolic of the finality of their separation. As Leonard's birth takes Ruth out of herself and teaches her to regret her actions more than her abandonment and to begin to see Bellingham for what he really is, the semiotics of clothing instantiate her belated self-awareness. For Gaskell, then, domestic details and clothing are crucial and complex aspects of characterization, but the seemingly self-evident black-and-white language of dress is complicated by both the textiles' origin and their history.

Not until the bulk of cotton textiles were understood to be of English origin could any cotton fabric be read as virtuous. Victorian commentators, eager to promote England's largest and "most important industry," began to argue that the introduction of cotton textiles had had, historically, a positive effect on English culture.[56] An article in *Chambers's Journal* titled "Cotton" makes this extraordinary claim for the days prior to cotton's introduction.

The poor were obliged to wear under-clothing of canvas, of woollen that could seldom be changed, and rarely washed, or too often to go without altogether. This last alternative was fearfully common, and helps to account for much of the disease and loathsome afflictions which were endemic among the poor.[57]

In this passage, the lack of cotton undergarments is historically refashioned as having induced disease, despite the fact that cotton itself was figured as a contagion upon the lower classes when it first became popular in England. The article may be read as suggesting, however, that celebrations of cotton's salubrious effects on the health and morals of Britons are appropriate only because the Indian competition has been vanquished, because the English suffer "no more dependence on Benares, Surat, Dacca, for the calicoes that every year made more valuable to consumers, whose love for decency, neatness, and cleanliness yearly increased."[58] Once the love of new clothing has been equated with a love of decency, neatness, and cleanliness, and the acquisition of cotton garments with the vanquishing of disease, the Manchester textile market may well concede a few special-occasion dresses to the "supple-handed Hindu" whose product is "superior . . . to the best productions of a machine." Such competition is in fact no threat because "the handicraft, with all its delicacy of execution, [is] a fossil" and will never again compete seriously with cheaper, machine-made English goods.[59] Dacca muslin's reputation is strengthened by the fact that cheap imitations are widely available; it is both celebrated as the fragile and valuable "'woven wind' of Bengal" and completely identified with English womanhood.[60] In an 1857 article in *Dublin University Magazine* titled "The Cotton Fields of India," the tone is half boastful, half elegiac: "The striped and figured muslins of Dacca, so long celebrated for the beauty and delicacy of their fabric, are now almost entirely displaced by the productions of Manchester and Paisley."[61] Furthermore, the demise of handloom weaving is frequently seen as beneficial to the health of textile workers. A typical statement of this kind may be found in an article in the *Edinburgh Review* written by Philip Meadows Taylor, the colonial administrator and novelist (who worked not for the British but for the rulers of Hyderabad), titled "Indian Costumes and Textile Fabrics." The article is ostensibly a review of *The Textile Manufacturers and the Costumes of the People of India,* by J. Forbes Watson,[62] "Reporter on the products of India to the

Secretary of State for India in Council";[63] in it, Taylor compares the darkened rooms in which the Dacca spinners supposedly sit to the conditions under which Brussels lace, another endangered handicraft, is spun,[64] thus implicitly suggesting that the one is as deleterious to the eyesight as the other (that Brussels lace was purchased at the price of its producers' vision was a Victorian commonplace).[65]

Paradoxically, however, *muslin* turns up regularly if not frequently in the nineteenth century as a disparaging slang term for "woman." The OED cites three examples, from Moncrieff's *Tom and Jerry* ("you've got a bit of muslin on the sly, have you?"), Thackeray's *Pendennis* ("that was a pretty bit of muslin hanging on your arm—who was she?"), and H. Smart's *From Post to Finish* ("keep clear of muslin for the next six or seven years. It's brought as many of your profession to grief as spirits"). All three citations appear to represent male-male interactions in which the "muslin" seems to be behaving, or be expected to behave, in ways that are more or less indecent. The signifier of both the wearer's purity and the weaver's "cunning," subtlety, and patience is, in these contexts, sexualized and made to evoke the barest hint of danger.[66] Calling a woman "muslin," like calling her a "skirt," is on one level simply metonymy—naming her in terms of something with which she is closely identified. But as the magazine articles' descriptions of the weavers remind us, muslin in the Victorian imagination is never far from the loom on which it was woven. The women identified as bits of muslin in these citations seem to be weaving webs in which to entangle unsuspecting men, whether by sneaking around with them, clinging to them, or distracting them from their duties,[67] and despite its unfamiliarity to us as a slang term, *muslin* in these contexts carries the force of a slur. The gendered trace of origin, seemingly vanquished by a novelistic parade of virginal Lucilla Marjoribanks lookalikes in their high white muslin dresses, reappears unexpectedly.

The so-called industrial novels raise another set of questions vis-à-vis textiles. In industrial novels, the industry in question is likely to be a cotton mill;[68] as Silver demonstrates, the existence of such mills depended on their ability to buy raw cotton from abroad (usually the United States) and to sell much of what they produced overseas as well. Yet in their attempts to make industry as English as the country house or the streets of London, novelists generally leave the international aspect of the textile trade out of their work. While industrial novels may work to naturalize the English factory system, this is not to say that they uncritically celebrate industry; clearly, one of their concerns is to critique it, as I discuss in my reading of *North and South* in chapter 1. But the very critiques generally presuppose the existence of factories and factory workers as a now-permanent part of the landscape that must be brought into line with a reformist ethos that permits workers to be exploited, but not too much. In *The Industrial Reformation of English Fiction,* Catherine Gallagher foregrounds the questions of slavery and abolition in the United States as they impacted the Manchester cotton trade and the Quakers who held such a prominent place in it. Manchester's relationship to India is similarly worth examining alongside the novels for the light it sheds both on the political philosophy of these captains of industry and on the omissions that structure the industrial novels themselves.

Elizabeth Stone's 1842 novel *William Langshawe, The Cotton Lord* is clearly a precursor to and an influence on Gaskell's *Mary Barton,*[69] but despite the fact that it is often classed as a "condition of England" novel, Stone is far more concerned with the condition of her characters' romantic fortunes. The melodramatic plot centers on Langshawe's daughter Edith; her self-made father disapproves of Frank Walmsley, the man she loves, and wishes to marry her off to the son of an old friend and business associate, Mr. Balshawe. Unbeknownst to Langshawe, the younger Balshawe is a "low-lived libertine"[70] who has seduced many factory girls, including a cousin of the Langshawe family. Commerce only enters the picture when it serves the exigencies of story: a speculation of Langshawe's fails, and Balshawe senior refuses to lend him money unless their children wed. On the verge of being sold into a dismal marriage, Edith is rescued at the altar by a hermit whom she'd befriended as a child; the hermit reveals her fiancé's wrongdoings, and Edith is spared marrying the man who has ruined her cousin. Despite Stone's references to cotton mills and the "cottonocracy," then, she evinces little interest in the industry *as* industry; when cotton does not appear as a mystical entity, as I discuss below, it is always already converted either into Marx's universal equivalent, money, or into commodities with which the cotton masters' "vulgar" wives gaudily decorate their homes.[71]

In *Capital,* Marx describes two ways in which commodities circulate under mercantile capitalism: the simplest form, C-M-C, represents "the transformation of commodities into money and the re-conversion of money back again into commodities: selling in order to buy."[72] This form of exchange is represented in *William Langshawe* by the domestic or household economy, in which the cotton masters sell their textiles (off-stage, naturally) and turn a portion of their profits over to their wives, who are responsible for broadcasting and upholding their families' status through the creation of specific kinds of domestic space.[73] The other form of exchange, M-C-M, represents the "the transformation of money into commodities, and the re-conversion of commodities into money: buying in order to sell."[74] As opposed to C-M-C, a closed equation in which the money is spent "once for all," the operation M-C-M is open-ended and, if properly performed, results in an ever-increasing cash flow: exchanging £100 for £110, then £110 for £120, and so forth. This type of iterated exchange is the domain of the masculine in *William Langshawe*, but even here, the issue of money is never central and is frequently elided; for example, Stone refers to a mythical Manchester cotton master as "Cotton-bags"[75] rather than the more common "money-bags." The novel celebrates manufacturing and mercantile capitalism in the abstract, but both are peripheral to the story; rather, Stone repeatedly personifies cotton, celebrating it fancifully as "the presiding genius of our district . . . to whom Aladdin's sprite was a nonentity,"[76] a "mighty potentate,"[77] and the common parent of the cotton lords.[78]

Critics have long recognized that Stone's overarching purpose in telling her tale is to redeem the Cottonocracy from charges of vulgarity and excessive interest in trade; in a survey of condition-of-England novels, Graham Law writes,

> To put it at its crudest, we can sketch three broadly articulated positions in published reactions to the process of industrialization in early Victorian England: "positive," "negative," and "mixed". . . . The "positive" response, which characteristically sees the mechanization of labour as the vanguard of scientific, material, social, and moral progress . . . finds its closest allies in those bourgeois manufacturing interests known as the Manchester School.[79]

Law classes *William Langshawe* as a "positive" response that is "unapologetically partisan in pleading the cause of long-suffering industrialists in the face of the ignorance and malice of their workers' representatives,"[80] as opposed to the mixed or ameliorist response that argues for "the long-term economic and social benefits of industrialization together with the assumption of some degree of responsibility for the short-term detrimental effects on the lives of workers."[81] In her witty evisceration of the novel, Rosemarie Bodenheimer notes that Stone bizarrely sets out to defend nouveau-riche Manchester from the snobbery of the landed classes by adopting the latter's standards of judgment. Stone attempts to perform this impossible task by "transforming Manchester society into a generator of genteel emotion and sentimental melodrama."[82] In so doing, Bodenheimer observes, "Her romantic conventionalities simply wipe out the offending factories and railways."[83] They also wipe out any sense of either the process or the product of the cotton mills, and the sense of circulation so crucial to other industrial novels is entirely absent. In this genteel vein, Frank Walmsley's wealthy uncle and guardian, who eventually provides the loan that rescues Langshawe, explains to Frank why he too disapproves of a match between Frank and Edith.

> My objection is not to [Edith], but to her family. . . . Far be it from me to depreciate Mrs. Langshawe's actual worth . . . [but] she is vulgarity personified; and smoothly as you may gloss over the circumstance *now,* your cheek would glow, and your fingers would tingle, Frank, to have this lady expatiating at your table with the freedom of a near relative. Mr. Langshawe is a shrewd and worldly man; his calculating head and his busy fingers have told a golden tale for him; but his heart and soul are wrapt in his counting-house and ledger. . . . Hand-in-hand with riches I have striven to gain those habitudes, tastes, and acquirements which alone can make riches respectable. Night after night, for weary hours after a day of toil, have I laboured as intently at mental acquirements as during daylight hours I have at the business of the countinghouse. . . . Whilst Mr. Langshawe and others of my compeers closed the day by a social meeting at a tavern, or by a domestic debauch.[84]

Eventually, of course, both he and Langshawe are proven wrong; Langshawe chooses disastrously for his daughter, and Frank, believing Edith to be married to Balshawe, marries a sixteen-year-old Italian girl for honor's sake after she and her English grandfather mistake his friendly intentions for romantic ones. In one of the novel's few unconventional (or just badly plotted?) moments, the Italian wife's death from consumption late in the narrative leaves the still-devoted lovers' plot unfinished if transparent in its apparent trajectory. Yet the resolution imperceptibly shifts to settle on Langshawe: he learns how better to value his daughter, and he becomes the novel's center of value, the successful capitalist and man of business, while Edith remains suspended in a state of spinsterhood, and Frank's uncle remains no wiser or better off for his hard-won gentlemanliness. The centrality of the aborted marriage plot cannot be overemphasized; it takes up most of the book, while the subplot involving the weavers' union escapes utter superfluity only in that the two-dimensional evil of the union operatives contrasts the paternal benevolence of the cotton lords (union members murder a cotton master's son in the penultimate chapter, an episode inspired by the 1831 murder of Thomas Ashton, which Gaskell also used in *Mary Barton*). Mill workers' grievances are not coded as false consciousness, as in *Mary Barton*, but as pure bad faith, urged on by their enablers in the press.

> While the orators of the political clubs and the scribes of the Radical newspaper press were declaiming on the slavery and the long-protracted toil of the factory operative—whilst ill-judging "philanthropists" were sighing over the much-exaggerated sorrows of the manufacturing labourers, these same people were not only devoting the night-hours, which, it might be imagined, with "slaves, o'erworn with toil," were best and naturally given to the pillow,—to midnight meetings of committees and delegates, but they were absolutely giving weekly, systematically, and readily, a considerable portion of the money "wrung from their sinews" to support all the arrangements of a "Trade's Union," with its liberally-stipended secretaries, delegates, and treasurers, and rout of inferior officers.[85]

In other words, the very existence of a union is proof not that the workers are sufficiently aggrieved to organize at the cost of their own time and money, but proof instead that they are overpaid, underworked, and greedy. As in Trollope's *Eustace Diamonds,* the implications of who is fit to command capital are clear. Yet because Stone's project is to humanize, if not romanticize, the cotton masters in the popular imagination and to defend the factory system wholesale, the laborers must be demonized and the actual work of textile-making occulted; Stone blithely dismisses any criticism of the mills by asserting that concerns regarding workers' health "originated in a state of things which now no longer exists."[86] Although Robert Peel appears briefly in the novel to praise Manchester's influence "in the scale of the empire,"[87] and Stone uncharacteristically but tellingly claims that "the *native* population of [Manchester], through all its grades, will bear comparison with any in the empire for vigour of intellect,"[88] the actual world outside Manchester is figured only by an absurdly romanticized Italy and a single Bengal tiger at a sideshow, and the "empire," with its presumably unvigorous and uncompetitive handloom weavers, is nowhere to be seen. The novel's eschewal of the global, that is, is of a piece with its refusal to confront the local; for even so conservative a reader of Manchester as Disraeli, as we will see, thinking the industrial landscape necessarily means thinking about India.

Disraeli's *Sybil* is generally understood to be a work whose purpose is to promulgate Disraeli's political vision, the core of which is the need for a genuinely superior aristocracy under whose influence a social compact between rich and poor may be effected. Once the members of each level of society understand and accept the duties incumbent upon their station, Disraeli argues, exploitation will diminish and the breach between rich and poor will begin to heal. To illustrate the causes and effects of England's malaise, Disraeli uses Manchester and India as privileged examples. Yet in Disraeli's vision, India belongs largely to the past, and cotton belongs solely to England. *Sybil* argues that much of England's aristocracy is not truly noble; titles have been and continue to be obtained by adventurers whose descendants therefore have no hereditary sense of how to discharge their responsibilities to their social inferiors. To demonstrate his point, Disraeli contrasts the present-day quest of Sir Vavasour Firebrace to purchase a new title with two parallel histories of noble families, one dating to the sixteenth century, one to the late eighteenth. The first history, that of Charles Egremont's ancestor Greymount, reveals Marney Abbey and the title of Lord Marney to have been the reward bestowed upon Henry VIII's most ruthless and rapacious despoiler of Church property. Charles Egremont's family, despite its Normanized name and despite being, in 1845, part of the "old" aristocracy, is revealed to be no more authentic than the clearly arriviste Fitz-Warenes, the second family whose ascent Disraeli traces.

The originator of the Fitz-Warene dynasty is an ambitious London club waiter named Warren who seizes an opportunity to travel to Bengal as the secretary to a newly appointed colonial administrator. Once there, having taken on most of his employer's duties, Warren makes his fortune-founding move: he buys up large stores of rice in anticipation of a famine, thus helping to precipitate it. When the food shortage has reached crisis level, Warren sells his hoarded grain back to the people at inflated prices. A few other such ventures allow him to return to England and purchase land, a seat in Parliament, and, eventually, a title.

In sketching this history, Disraeli maintains a telegraphic style and a tone of dry understatement that contrast markedly with his sentimental depictions of the English working classes and especially of Sybil and Walter Gerard. Understatement is, in Disraeli's work, inevitably the tone of attack.

> [Warren's] master went out to make a fortune; but he was indolent, and had indeed none of the qualities for success, except his great position. Warren had every quality but that. The basis of the confederacy therefore was intelligible; it was founded on mutual interests and cemented by reciprocal assistance. The governor granted monopolies to the secretary, who apportioned a due share to his sleeping partner. There appeared one of those dearths not unusual in Hindostan; the population of the famished province cried out for rice; the stores of which, diminished by nature, had for months mysteriously disappeared. A provident administration it seems had invested the public revenue in its benevolent purchase; the misery was so excessive that even pestilence was anticipated, when the great forestallers came to the rescue of the people over whose destinies they presided; and at the same time fed, and pocketed, millions.[89]

In the character of Charles Egremont, Disraeli seems to suggest that such tainted roots may be transcended through the adoption of correct attitudes and actions toward the poor and the working classes. As in *Coningsby*, when the aristocrat Eustace Lyle puts in place a system of manorial caretaking for those left out of the industrial economy, the relation Disraeli sets up between rich and poor leaves aside all implications of the international economy in which all sides are increasingly bound up.[90] The ethics of mill (or mine) ownership, in this system, begin and end with the owners' responsibility to the workers they employ. So the dishonest practices of the mill owners Shuffle and Screw are contrasted with the enlightened system put in place by Trafford, who provides education as well as a safe workplace to his employees. Although the desperate situation of the displaced handloom weaver Philip Warner would seem to disrupt this system and open the possibility of acknowledging the similar fate of displaced Indian weavers, the implications of Warner's travails are never developed. His problems are folded back into the framework of the aristocracy's duty to the peasantry. So it is fitting that Sybil, as the representative of the true nobility who is also one of "the people," is the source of Warner's relief, as I discuss in chapter 4.

Yet *Sybil* repeatedly engages with ideas about India, cotton, and weavers, if not with Indian cotton or Indian weavers. Furthermore, the tommy-shop episodes that describe how miners' families are forced to buy food from the mine owners may be linked thematically to the story of Warren and the rice famine. Even as he condemns the industrialists for exploiting the poor, Disraeli suggests that Warren's Indian crimes continue to haunt him after his return to England. The absent presence of India glimmers to the surface as well when Disraeli uses India to make points about domestic affairs; to illustrate what is wrong with England, Disraeli at many moments holds up India as a mirror—sometimes in passing, sometimes at length. In noting the inability of the English poor to provide for their offspring, for example, he remarks, "Infanticide is practiced as extensively and as legally in England, as it is on the banks of the Ganges; a circumstance which apparently has not yet engaged the attention of the Society for the Propagation of the Gospel in Foreign Parts."[91] Yet Disraeli's statement that the eighteenth century was the century in which India mattered, and that the French Revolution "turned the public attention for ever from Indian affairs,"[92] suggests the degree to which even his early writings had begun to sound the theme upon which he expounded so famously in his 1872 Crystal Palace speech, that England was indifferent to its empire.

Manchester, however, had never lost sight of India; Peter Harnetty argues that the Manchester cotton masters viewed India consistently throughout the nineteenth century as "a vast market for their products [that] they were determined to capture and exploit . . . to the greatest extent possible," securing for themselves in 1814 a system of tariff duties that "allowed British manufactures to enter India at a nominal rate, permitted raw cotton to leave India at a nominal duty, but retained the high British tariffs which put Indian cotton manufactures at a considerable disadvantage in the British market."[93] During the forty-five-year period between 1814 and 1859, pressure from cotton manufacturers kept these low tariffs in place despite the fact that the British government in India incurred massive debt. Manchester's interests were represented in Parliament by Richard Cobden and John Bright; their leadership of the Anti-Corn Law League has indelibly associated them with the cause of free trade, but in reality, throughout the 1830s and 1840s Manchester supported various measures to increase the production of raw cotton in India.[94] Manchester's efforts to encourage the cultivation of Indian cotton made great strides after Berar and Nagpur were annexed in 1853 "specifically with an eye to their cotton-producing potential."[95] Disraeli's contrast of corrupt East India Company functionaries and industrialists appears to elide the fact that the source of their revenue is the same, yet the very juxtaposition of the two suggests the connection.

To return, by way of conclusion, to the domestic novel: to a degree unusual in such works, Indian material culture as such is very much on display in Charlotte Yonge's *The Clever Woman of the Family*, a novel that may be said to prefigure the conservative assaults on the "New Woman" of the 1880s and 1890s. Yonge's interweaving of civilian and military life both structures the narrative and underpins the theme of masculine influence on women's moral education, the lack of which is frequently cited by Ermine Williams, the novel's actual Clever Woman, as the source of would-be clever Rachel Curtis's problems. Rachel wants to be a moral force in her community but does not know how because she has no male examples or teachers; as a result, she merely makes a nuisance of herself until her ill-advised scheme to found a charity school causes the death of a child and she is held responsible. She had desired to rescue girls from a lacemaking school, but her own school is far worse.[96] Universally condemned and publicly shamed, Rachel has a breakdown but is rehabilitated by Captain Alick Keith, the war hero who sees through her folly but loves her regardless. Humbled into giving up her self-aggrandizing schemes, Rachel finally begins to realize her dream of actually doing good by acting as assistant to Alick's blind uncle, a clergyman. His influence teaches her that

> many of her errors had chiefly arisen from the want of some one whose superiority she could feel, and her old presumptions withered up to nothing when she measured her own powers with those of a highly educated man, while all the time he gave her thanks and credit for all she had effected, but such as taught her humility by very force of infection.[97]

The novel opens as the military men quartered at Avoncester, the "__th Highlanders,"[98] have returned to England from duty in Australia and India, where they fought to suppress what the novel terms the Mutiny of 1857. The former commanding officer, the father of Captain Alick Keith and Bessie Keith, was mortally wounded at Lucknow; the bodies of the younger members of the clan have been indelibly marked by the Mutiny. Alick has lost part of his hand at the siege of Delhi; his cousin Colin Keith, Ermine's fiancé, has a bullet lodged in his chest.[99] For the women, conversely, the Indian sojourn seems to have produced only luxuries and nostalgia. At the Gowanbrae ball that celebrates the men's return, the coatroom overflows with "cashmere cloaklets,"[100] and Bessie wears in her hair "an eagle's feather clasped in it by a large emerald, a memory of her father's last siege—that of Lucknow."[101] When Colin Keith tells Ermine's niece that she will have "a grand exhibition of my Indian curiosities," she replies, "Have you Indian curiosities? I thought they were only for ladies?"[102] (His response: "perhaps they are.") Reduced to miniatures and locked in a cabinet, India is produced not as an object of knowledge but of sentiment and sensation, appropriate for women and small children.

In her eagerness to prove her moral and intellectual superiority to the women around her, Rachel falls prey to a criminal named Maddox, who previously ruined the Williams family financially and socially by stealing their money with forged documents and pinning the blame on Ermine's brother. Rachel tells Maddox of her desire to found a school, and he encourages her to raise funds, claiming that he knows a respectable teacher who can run the school in a house some distance away. This woman is his longtime accomplice Maria Hatherton, who performs the role of benevolent headmistress for visitors to the school and otherwise systematically starves, beats, and terrorizes her "pupils" until they are rescued by Fanny Temple, who is newly arrived in town with the returning troops. Fanny, a general's widow and commander of her own troop of six boys, who has earned Rachel's contempt for her youthfulness and meekness, goes on a routine visit, deduces immediately that something is gravely wrong, and proceeds to rescue the pupils by outmaneuvering Maria Hatherton with bold military tactics.

Maria Hatherton is repeatedly linked with the rebellious Indian troops that Fanny's husband vanquished; even before her crimes are discovered, Colin Keith tells Rachel that Maria calls to mind "a face I saw in India . . . a very handsome Sepoy havildar whom we took at Lucknow; a capital soldier before the mutiny, and then an ineffable ruffian."[103] (This history parallels Maria's; she was a respectable servant and favorite of the Williams family until she fell in with Maddox and helped him to ruin them.) In one of many examples of Rachel's refusal to pay attention to straightforward evidence, she tartly replies, "The mutiny was an infectious frenzy; so that you establish nothing against that cast of countenance."[104] Fanny's son Conrade, who has witnessed the rescue, cries out to Rachel, "Oh, Aunt Rachel, your [charity school] is as bad as the Sepoys. But we have saved the two little girls they were whipping to death."[105] When Rachel tells Alick Keith that Maddox was out solely for financial gain and "it was only the woman that was cruel," he replies grimly, "she had not her Sepoy face for nothing."[106]

The Clever Woman of the Family is unusual among domestic novels even for veering so close to an outright representation of Indian affairs, jingoistic as it is; even so, when the men's defining battle is restaged by the women on domestic turf, the part of the evil opponent is played by a woman who looks, and by extension acts, like a "Sepoy," but who is in fact English.[107] The women's relationship to India, which remains a point of narrative reference throughout the novel, is always mediated, in this case through an imagined relationship to an imaginary Indian identity, but more often through material objects.

Yet finally, Indian textiles stand in neither for Indian people nor for India itself in any direct or uncomplicated way. Rachel's unpleasant personality traits—she is universally perceived to be bossy, argumentative, and judgmental—are mirrored by her personal appearance, a hallmark of which is her "severely simple and practical"[108] taste in clothing. She only agrees to attend the Gowanbrae ball with the stipulation that she wear a dinner dress rather than a ball gown, an eccentricity to which her peers are acclimated: "indeed the county was pretty well accustomed to Miss Rachel Curtis's ball-room ways, and took them as a matter of course."[109] Her transformation, effected by a series of crushing humiliations and capped by the death of one of her charity-school pupils, is enacted sartorially as she recovers from her breakdown with her new husband Alick at his blind uncle's home. She has been avoiding society, aware that she has been harshly judged, but finds herself compelled at last to attend a party and resolves to behave in a new way because she owes it to her husband to do so.

> Ermine's hint, that with Rachel it rested to prevent her unpopularity from injuring her husband, had not been thrown away, and she never manifested any shrinking from the party, and even took some interest in arraying herself for it.
>
> "That is what I call well turned out," exclaimed Alick, when she came down.
>
> "Describe her dress, if you please," said Mr. Clare; "I like to hear how my nieces look."
>
> Alick guided his hand. . . . "is it Grace's taste, Rachel? for it is the

prettiest thing you have worn—a pale buff sort of silky thing, embroidered all over in the same colour;" and he put a fold of the dress into his uncle's hand.

"Indian, surely," said Mr. Clare, feeling the pattern; "it is too intricate and graceful for the West."[110]

Once again, Rachel is caught up in the historical text that has been woven between the lines of the plot. Having clothed herself in submission and penitence, much like the "oriental woman" of Victorian fantasy, she becomes not more spiritual or intellectual but more corporeal. She functions as Mr. Clare's eyes and Alick's hand, and in this scene performs another service for her husband by using her clothed self to translate India from a scene of bloodshed and loss into something intricate and graceful that delights him. The fabric, so distinctive as to be identifiable by touch alone, bears the marks of the embroidery needle and thus connects Rachel to the idea of women's work, but it also speaks of display and frivolity, women's weaknesses. Prior to her transformation, Rachel's problem was not that she was flawed but that her flaws were masculine—ambition and the desire for public acclaim. The dress reconfigures her within an acceptably gendered realm of feminine error (her sister's mildly excessive interest in clothes). By willingly identifying herself with the dress, Rachel demonstrates that she has learned the value of being contained and controlled, of submitting to the tutelage of superior authority. That is, the graceful Indian textile represents her reformed state, but also her having been in need of reform. Yet the textile itself does not exactly or completely submit to this logic; it is not "too intricate and graceful to be Western," but "too intricate and graceful for the West." It thus resists complete identification with Rachel, who may now be good but who is neither intricate nor graceful, and with the project of domestication in which it participates. Its own excess of signification (too intricate) suggests that as a commodity produced for foreign consumption, it both anticipates and complicates the fantasies that are pressed upon it. As in domestic novels in which young women body forth their virtue in white Dacca muslin, and in industrial novels about displaced handloom weavers and abused factory hands, India is not merely context but intertext: rather than functioning as the backdrop to these narratives of English identity, India is the warp thread that connects them.

CHAPTER THREE

Plunder as Property: Diamonds

It is perhaps becoming clear that to follow various South Asian commodities back to their points of origin is frequently to find territorial conflict if not outright war. In this sense, Indian diamonds are no different, although their mythology is perhaps the most elaborate and overdetermined of any commodity in this study. In the Victorian popular imagination, diamonds were associated with India, particularly south India, which, until diamonds were discovered in Brazil and Borneo around 1725, was Europe's sole source. (With a few exceptions, India remained the world's sole source of large diamonds until the advent of commercial mining in South Africa around 1870.) Diamonds were being cut and polished in the Indus valley as early as the third century B.C.E., when Chanakya's *Arthasastra,* an economics text in which the industry is described, was written. Diamonds are also mentioned in early South Asian epics, scriptures, and gemology treatises and were known in Europe at least from the first century C.E.[1] In his *Natural History,* Pliny the Elder gives a fanciful account of an Indian jungle floor virtually paved with diamonds. Such stories were fueled by the fact that Indian diamonds were found close to the earth's surface in alluvial rather than hard-rock beds, and mining therefore consisted primarily of digging pits or raking the earth followed by endless sifting, rather than underground tunneling.

European travelers and merchants of the seventeenth century, when the Indian diamond industry was at its peak, have left accounts of the trade, of which the French jeweler and diamond merchant Jean Baptiste Tavernier's (1605–89) *Les Six Voyages de Jean Baptiste Tavernier* is probably the best known. Tavernier's great Indian purchase was the 112-carat blue diamond that would become known as the Hope Diamond.[2] His travel narrative describes Golconda, an ancient city near what is now Hyderabad and the then-capital of the Kutub Shahi rulers, as the center of diamond cutting and trading, and it is from these accounts that the entire range of geographically disparate South Indian mines came to be known generally as the Golconda Diamond Mines. As used in Europe, the name Golconda thus registers a dreamscape of riches rather than a geographic specificity.

While Brazilian diamonds were abundant, they were small in size compared to those found in India; their discovery by European merchants paved the way for a socially downward movement of the diamond trade toward the upper middle class in the nineteenth century.[3] Nevertheless, India continued to reign in the English imagination as a seat of fabulous gemstone riches, a fantasy fueled as much by the actual non-diamond-related fortunes amassed by East India Company functionaries as by such occasional finds as the 340-carat Nizam diamond in 1835.[4]

Wilkie Collins's 1868 novel *The Moonstone* is predicated on events involving two historical figures who at first glance have little directly to do with the diamond trade: Tipu Sultan and his father Hyder Ali, Muslim rulers of the kingdom of Mysore in the second half of the eighteenth century. Hyder Ali was a legendary figure who went from holding an independent command in Mysore to deposing the rajah and naming himself leader in 1761. A 1767 alliance of the British, Marathas, and the Nizam of Hyderabad failed to unseat him in the first of four Anglo-Mysore wars, and Hyder continued to battle the British army for control of south India until his death in 1782 during the second Anglo-Mysore war (1780–84). His son Tipu assumed the throne and fought two subsequent wars; Tipu was killed in battle at the fall of Seringapatam (now Srirangapatna) during the fourth and final Anglo-Mysore war in 1799. The Anglo-Mysore wars had a curious afterlife in early-nineteenth-century culture; the rulers' military prowess, the splendor of their court, and their reputation for cruelty to their prisoners of war fascinated and repelled the English, as did the dramatic story of the fall of Seringapatam and the discovery of Tipu's body by General David Baird, a Scottish officer who had previously been Tipu's prisoner. Tipu's death was widely written about, and the capture of Srirangapatam was illustrated by such painters as

Alexander Allan, Henry Singleton, J. M. W. Turner, and Sir David Wilkie, Collins's godfather.[5]

An early literary use of Hyder Ali and Tipu is seen in Walter Scott's 1827 novella *The Surgeon's Daughter,* one of the stories that comprise the first series of the *Chronicles of the Canongate.* As Molly Youngkin has noted, few critics have bothered to analyze this minor work other than to enumerate its failings.[6] Yet Scott's fictional treatment of historical figures in this context is worth examining for the light it sheds on the complexity of the British response to the fall of Seringapatam and the way it prefigures the intricately gendered conflation of property, plunder, and capital in Collins and, I will argue, in Anthony Trollope's 1871 novel *The Eustace Diamonds.*

At the risk of stating the obvious, Scott is known both for his historical novels and his framing devices, and *The Surgeon's Daughter* is doubly framed so as to vex considerably the question of history. In his introduction, Scott (writing as himself) informs his readers that "the principal incident" in the story (the sale of a Scottish woman to an Indian man by her fiancé) was narrated to him by his friend Joseph Train, the antiquary from whom Scott had in the past derived source material on Scotland, including, as he notes in his introduction to the *Chronicles,* the history of Old Mortality.[7] Furthermore, he notes, his source for "information as to Indian matters" was "Colonel James Ferguson of Huntley Burn, one of the sons of the venerable historian of that name."[8] Following the introduction in the 1855 edition of the *Chronicles* is an appendix consisting of Train's written version of the story he'd narrated to Scott, which, the editors explain, was requested by Scott but "did not reach Abbotsford until July 1832," that is to say, shortly before Scott's death in September of that year.

In chapter 1 of *The Surgeon's Daughter,* however, the narrator, as in the previous chronicles, is named as the comically absurd Mr. Chrystal Croftangry; he begins by describing the reaction of his friend Mr. Fairscribe to the first two tales in the *Chronicles* (*The Highland Widow* and *The Two Drovers*). Fairscribe pronounces them better than "Shiller's [*sic*]," because "a book of amusement should be something that one can take up and lay down at pleasure; and I can say justly, I was never at the least loss to put aside these sheets of yours," whereas Schiller "does not let you off so easily."[9] Fairscribe then suggests that Croftangry should "do with your Muse of Fiction, as you call her, as many an honest man has done with his own sons in flesh and blood": send her to India.[10] When Croftangry protests that he knows nothing whatever of India, his friend replies that "you will tell us about them all the better that you know nothing of what you are saying" and volunteers his daughter to recount to Croftangry the tale of his distant relation, "poor Menie Grey," who was betrayed by her lover and nearly sold to an Indian rajah.[11] Chapter 2 commences Croftangry's rendering of the story, and the tale concludes with his reading his work before a ladies' tea party, where the "mention of shawls, diamonds, turbans, and cummerbunds, had their usual effect in awakening the imaginations" of his auditors.[12]

Thus Scott has it both ways: the author's truth-claims are countered by the narrator's assertion that he has invented everything but the bare bones of the story, yet the stark differences between the terse four-page narrative attributed to Train and the fictional Croftangry's expansive story would seem to support Scott's contention that the account mediates truth and fiction, despite the fact that the story has all the hallmarks of being what a twenty-first-century reader would call an urban legend (it lacks names, places, or dates).[13] What is strikingly absent from Train's account, however, is any mention of Tipu Sultan or Hyder Ali; rather, it is an anonymous "native Rajah" who has fallen in love with a miniature portrait of Emma, the surgeon's daughter, and contracted to buy her from the treacherous Scottish lover who decoys her to India with the promise of marriage.[14] Only the assiduous attentions of her ship's captain, an old schoolfellow of her brother, save her from her fate.

Why, then, does Scott introduce Tipu and Hyder Ali? Perhaps in part because this is a story about wealth, inheritance, and diamonds; a diamond ring is the only tangible link Richard Middlemas, the man who eventually attempts to sell his fiancé to "Tippoo," has to his unmarried mother, who abandoned him at birth. Adopted by the Scottish doctor who delivered him and raised on his nurse's stories of his birth mother's beauty and fortune, Middlemas learns at fourteen that his mother was Jewish and Portuguese and his father an English Catholic Jacobite; furthermore, his parents' whereabouts are unknown, and his wealthy and powerful maternal grandfather, who has paid for his upbringing, wants nothing to do with him. Embittered by this knowledge, Middlemas rejects the chance to assume his adoptive father's medical practice and marry Menie, his stepsister and first love, choosing instead to seek his fortune with the East India

Company in the belief that India is a place "where gold is won by steel; where a brave man cannot pitch his desire of fame and wealth so high, but that he may realize it, if he have fortune to his friend!"[15]

Once in India, however, Middlemas disgraces himself by killing an officer in a duel, flees, and subsequently falls in with Tippoo, thus committing the crimes of "mutiny, murder, desertion, and serving of the enemy against his countrymen."[16] His attempts to make his fortune by alternately courting Tippoo and his followers, and plotting to betray him to the British in order to be pardoned for his crimes, culminate in a plan to lure Menie, herself described as "a gem—a diamond," to India by asking her to marry him.[17] Tippoo has fallen in love with Middlemas's miniature of her and wishes to make her his mistress, while Middlemas plans to betray Tippoo for a percentage of the "gold and diamonds" held in his fort at Bangalore.[18] Middlemas thus hopes to receive two shares of Tippoo's diamonds and gold: one for a Scottish woman, and another for betraying Tippoo's movements and plans to the British. In this bizarrely triangulated exchange, the only material commodity that is straightforwardly for sale is Menie Gray. In the story's climax, the hero Adam Hartley informs Tippoo's father Hyder Ali of his son's plot. Hyder, who as a good Muslim abhors his son's attempt to barter "justice for lust," intervenes by causing Middlemas to be trampled by an elephant, thus aborting the exchange by replacing it with another form of Indian barbarism.[19] Andrew Lincoln observes in his reading of *Guy Mannering* that in this earlier work, "to preserve the integrity of his hero, Scott must suppress the image of empire as an aggressive adventure driven by commercial gain with scant respect to the legitimacy of established regimes. Empire must be seen as a gentlemanly, civilizing project."[20] While *The Surgeon's Daughter* is more equivocal in some respects, certainly it participates in the same system of values that Lincoln unpacks.[21] Middlemas's problem is that his identity as he understands it is in perpetual conflict with his upbringing; unable either to accept his adopted father's solid Scottish Presbyterian values or to participate in his grandfather's mercantile empire, he fails as an imperialist by refusing to participate in the dominant order. His attempt to trade a European woman for diamonds violates all accepted methods of accumulating colonial wealth, yet the trope of bartering of gems for human "lives," in many senses of the word, reappears in mid-Victorian novels, often carrying with it the trace of colonial violence.

Critics have long argued that *The Eustace Diamonds* is in many respects a rewriting of *The Moonstone*. This line of reading appears to have begun with Henry James Wye Milley, who in a 1937 article worked out the novels' connections first in relation to the detective element and then in terms of parallel characters and plot points, augmenting his reading with quotations from Trollope's autobiography that demonstrate Trollope's fascinated and attentive distaste for Collins's style in general and *The Moonstone* in particular.[22] Detective elements aside, Milley makes clear that to the extent that Trollope did rewrite, he did so in his own idiom: what Trollope called in his autobiography the realistic,[23] rather than the sensation, novel.

It is perhaps for this reason that the stones that give each novel its name, the Eustace diamonds and the Moonstone, have been read by critics in strikingly different ways. *The Moonstone* begins with an incident based on an actual episode of looting during the siege of Srirangapatna (Seringapatam in the novel) in the fourth Anglo-Mysore war of 1799,[24] and the plot is driven at many points by Brahmin priests' pursuit of the diamond, which is restored to its ancestral home in the epilogue. Not surprisingly, then, *The Moonstone*'s diamonds tend to be viewed through the lens of British imperialism; the Eustace diamonds, conversely, have long been understood to embody a more domestic struggle for wealth, power, and status. More recently, *The Eustace Diamonds* has figured prominently in studies of Victorian novels' relation to commodity culture.[25] I wish to argue that Collins's and Trollope's diamonds have more in common than is first apparent, and that these commonalities shed light particularly on *The Eustace Diamonds*'s (and Trollope's perennial) themes of power, property, and patrimony. Victorian stories involving diamonds necessarily involve India, and Trollope acknowledges this fact, if obliquely; he uses a subplot involving an Indian property claim, a contest for a piece of the jewel in England's crown, to illuminate the dispute over Lizzie Eustace's diamond necklace. In eliminating the sensational Indians of Collins's text—those mysterious and murderous Brahmin priests—with characters more appropriate to realism—members of Parliament and undersecretaries of State—Trollope suggests that what was actually at stake for the British government as the aftermath of the fourth Anglo-Mysore war and the death of Tipu Sultan resonated late into the nineteenth century was the control of land and resources, matters that are obscured by the diamond mystery in *The Moonstone*.

Several critics have noted *The Moonstone's* complex relation to narratives of the Rebellion of 1857;[26] in some sense, these arguments suggest, the struggle to possess and define the Moonstone figures the contest in India.[27] *The Eustace Diamonds* shifts the ground somewhat by making the diamonds symbolic of English aristocratic wealth and power while drawing parallels between the diamonds and a shadowy case that looks very much like a contemporary claim for control of territory in Mysore partitioned by the British in the wake of Tipu's death. Papers relating to this case, which involved the rajah of Mysore, Krishnaraja Wodeyar III, who had been placed on the throne of Mysore by Lord Wellesley himself at the end of the fourth Anglo-Mysore war, were published in the Parliamentary Papers for 1867–68, where Trollope might certainly have encountered them. It is even more likely that, as a founder of *The Fortnightly Review* (in 1865), he would have known of a detailed article supporting the rajah's case written by John Morley and published there in 1866, shortly before Morley became its editor,[28] and five years before *The Eustace Diamonds* appeared in its pages.

If *The Eustace Diamonds's* imperial context seems opaque to us at this remove, it is in part because Trollope has replaced the specifically Indian commodity—the unmounted gemstone of Collins's story—with an enclosed and domesticated item of jewelry, the diamond necklace. Both novels, however, partake of a set of conventions that surround these converging fields of signification. The means by which foreign treasure becomes domestic jewelry, and the layers of meaning that are gained and shed in that process, are crucial to *The Eustace Diamonds's* thematization of diamonds. To understand the place of diamonds in culture, it is necessary to reconnect two strands of gendered thematic material that tend to be dissevered in Victorian literature. The first is the trope of jewelry-as-identification or identity, which is the province of the domestic novel, in which jewelry is understood to be property, and the second is the colonial treasure trove, found in the novel of adventure, in which gemstones are understood to be plunder. Once this link has been made, we can see how, even cut, mounted, and locked away in an English strongbox, diamonds can invoke England's vexed and vastly complicated relationship to India even as they illuminate class and gender axes of property ownership and the ways in which belief systems regarding who is fit to own and administer wealth come to possess the force of law.

In both the possession and the wearing, jewelry in Victorian novels tells tales: of origins, of status, of history. To name but a few examples: in Charles Dickens's 1838 novel *Oliver Twist,* Oliver's evil half-brother Monks drops a locket and ring that belonged to Oliver's mother into a river in the reasonable belief that doing so will obliterate any trace of Oliver's true identity. In Wilkie Collins's *Hide and Seek* (1854), the secret of Madonna Grice's origins is woven into a hair bracelet that contains two types of hair and two sets of initials; in an act of metonymic substitution, her adoptive father locks the bracelet away in order to assuage his pervasive fear that his daughter will be stolen from him. Similarly, in George Eliot's 1872 novel *Felix Holt,* a pair of engraved lockets with locks of hair secreted inside unlock the secret of Esther Lyon's birthright. Specific gems (which, like flowers, had a language of their own), mourning jewelry, hair jewelry, and even the presence of lace instead of jewelry are all meant to announce categories to which the wearer, bearer, owner, or giver belong.[29] Townspeople at the annual charity ball in *Wives and Daughters* are outraged that a visiting duchess fails to wear the parure of diamonds for which she is famous.[30] And in the poignant denouement of *Cranford,* the aged Miss Matty's long-lost brother, who has not seen her since she was a young woman, returns from India with a pearl necklace and muslin gown that she is far too old to wear.[31]

The conventional allure of jewelry—it is assumed both to signal the attraction of the wearer's wealth and to make her more beautiful to look at—was furthered by materials that, in addition to being costly, suggested the glamour of faraway places. Since a great percentage of the gemstones to be found in Victorian England originated in Asia, jewelry was subject to much fantasizing about its already-exoticized origins. Because Victorian women were assumed to wear gemstone ornaments more commonly than men (a point which itself should be historicized), they were therefore assumed in the popular imagination to desire jewelry and gems more than men. But the colonial treasure trove is, as a feminized quest-object, the province of male protagonists. These men, such tales suggest, desire the wealth, power, and status for which the jewels may be traded rather than the ornaments themselves, and they welcome the hardships attendant upon the struggle to win them. Aspects of this model may be seen in two paradigmatic novels of imperial adventure, Rudyard Kipling's *Jungle Books* and Rider Haggard's *King Solomon's Mines.* Both feature scenes in which the protagonists descend into womblike underground spaces and discover the forgotten treasure hoard of an ancient civilization.

Kipling takes us under the jungle floor in the second *Jungle Book* to suggest that in India, treasures crafted by humans are so plentiful and so thoroughly disowned or forgotten that they may be mined as easily as raw gems; Mowgli and his native informant, the cobra Kaa, enter the lair of the legendary white cobra and see, buried in "five or six feet" of loose gold coins that have burst free of rotted sacks,

> jewelled elephant-howdahs of embossed silver, studded with plates of hammered gold, and adorned with carbuncles and turquoises. There were palanquins and litters for carrying queens, framed and braced with silver and enamel, with jade-handled poles and amber curtain-rings; there were golden candlesticks hung with pierced emeralds that quivered on the branches; there were studded images, five feet high, of forgotten gods, silver with jewelled eyes; there were coats of mail, inlaid on steel, and fringed with rotted and blackened seed-pearls; there were helmets, crested and beaded with pigeon's-blood rubies; there were shields of lacquer, of tortoise-shell and rhinoceros-hide, strapped and bossed with red gold and set with emeralds at the edge; there were sheaves of diamond-hilted swords, daggers, and hunting-knives; there were golden sacrificial bowls and ladles, and portable altars of a shape that never sees the light of day; there were jade cups and bracelets; there were incense-burners, combs, and pots for perfume, henna, and eye-powder, all in embossed gold; there were nose-rings, armlets, headbands, finger-rings, and girdles past any counting; there were belts seven fingers broad, of square-cut diamonds and rubies, and wooden boxes, trebly clamped with iron, from which the wood had fallen away in powder, showing the pile of uncut star-sapphires, opals, cat's-eyes, sapphires, rubies, diamonds, emeralds, and garnets within.[32]

I quote at length in order to suggest the way in which this image of foreign treasure is itself extravagant to the story. Here, images of decadence and decay compete with an almost hallucinatory excess of timeless treasure; the bejeweled relics suggest a highly evolved society, but one in which the accoutrements of priestcraft and war have been feminized by their encrustation with gems. The gods are "forgotten," the strongboxes and bags decayed, and the white cobra doesn't know that the great city whose treasure he guards has long since returned to the jungle. Mowgli easily defeats the snake in a fight and humiliates him by prying his mouth open to reveal his impotence: his dreaded fangs have been reduced to rotted stumps and his poison sacs shriveled. Even as Mowgli protests that he has no interest whatever in the treasure since it cannot be eaten and is therefore not "good hunting," the reader is meant to be riveted by the overwhelming spectacle of "the sifted pickings of centuries of war, plunder, trade, and taxation," lying there unclaimed, waiting to be seized and made use of by the first man enterprising enough to find it.[33]

Mowgli, a boy-man like Kipling's Kim, is by virtue of his ability to assimilate into an alien culture the colonial adventurer par excellence; he effortlessly reveals the effeminacy and impotence of this archaic civilization and emerges triumphant with the phallic elephant-goad, a symbol of mastery over a dangerous but feminized nature. Anne McClintock elaborates on this theme of feminized colonial geography in her reading of the climactic mine-entering scene in H. Rider Haggard's *King Solomon's Mines.*

> Only Gagool [the ancient African witch] knows the secret entrance to the mines, a psychosexual image needing no elaboration. Entry to the narrow passage is guarded by huge, nude Phoenician colossi. Over the door of the treasure chamber the men read their racial patrimony, the title deed to ownership of the diamonds: "We stood and shrieked with laughter over the gems that had been found for *us* thousands of years ago and saved for *us* by Solomon's long-dead overseer. . . . We had got them." . . . What follows is an extraordinary fantasy of male birthing, culminating in the regeneration of white manhood. . . . According to this phantasmatic narrative of white patriarchal regeneration, the white men give birth to the new economic order of imperial mining capitalism.[34]

In this passage, McClintock limns the psychoanalytics of the mythic text while placing the myth into its historical element: late-nineteenth-century South Africa was indeed the locus of diamond-mining ventures on every scale that depended on vast amounts of heavily guarded native labor rather than witch guides and treasure maps. So while it is necessary to read texts like Haggard's and Kipling's in terms of the fact that European imperialists and military adventurers feminized the place-to-be-conquered in order to justify their mission, the treasure-gathering scenes themselves cannot be taken at face value, for such fantasies occlude more than they reveal about property, plunder, and profit in imperial enterprises.[35] While the looting of Indian treasures (and treasuries) was certainly real, dramatizations tended to deflect attention from the prosaic fact that a key source of wealth in India was labor power, once it was properly harnessed to the British cause. Speaking of treasure as simply being there for the individual's taking meant that the presence of mining and mining-related industries, which existed prior to British hegemony, need not be taken into account. It also meant that the conditions under which wealth was extracted from British-controlled industry, agriculture, taxation, and trade were displaced by the fantasy of stuffing one's pockets with riches; as Franco Moretti has written of *King Solomon's Mines,* "at the end of the journey . . . we don't find raw materials, or ivory, or human beings to be enslaved . . . [we find] a fairy-tale entity—a 'treasure'—where the bloody profits of the colonial adventure are sublimated into an aesthetic, almost self-referential object: glittering, *clean* stones."[36]

At the level of plot, then, the colonial treasure's only relation to that other popular Victorian treasure-trove, the wealthy woman's jewel-casket, is that both are the locus of an extraordinary amount of criminal activity. As Sherlock Holmes proclaims of the gem that gives its name to "The Blue Carbuncle,"

> Of course it is a nucleus and focus of crime. Every good stone is. They are the devil's pet baits. In the larger and older jewels every facet may stand for a bloody deed. This stone is not yet twenty years old. . . . In spite of its youth, it has already a sinister history. There have been two murders, a vitriol-throwing, a suicide, and several robberies brought about for the sake of this forty-grain weight of crystallized charcoal. Who would think that so pretty a toy would be a purveyor to the gallows and the prison?[37]

As Holmes suggests, part of the allure of an important gem is its history, even (or especially) a bloody one—but it is a history that in the domestic novel, as opposed to the adventure tale, begins once the gem has entered England and become the property of some noble house or other. The great counterexample, of course, is Collins's *The Moonstone.* It is perhaps the one instance in which, as the servant-narrator Gabriel Betteredge says, "our quiet English house [was] suddenly invaded by a devilish Indian Diamond"[38] that is explicitly marked as having brought with it a heavy freight of colonial baggage.

Although the diamonds in Anthony Trollope's 1872 novel *The Eustace*

Diamonds are once referred to as having come from the Golconda diamond mines, in the novel's terms they begin life in 1799, when they are written into the English legal record.[39] Lizzie's husband's grandfather, "on the occasion of his marriage," either sells or trades other gems "said to have been heirlooms" (I.149) for the diamonds in question, at which time they first appear in the Eustace family documents. As befits the understated action of a domestic novel, the initial crime in *The Eustace Diamonds* consists of nothing more than a gesture of refusal, bolstered by deft shading of the truth.[40] In fact, Sir Florian Eustace did indeed physically hand his family's diamond necklace to his lawfully wedded wife Lizzie Eustace with the intention that she wear it. After Sir Florian's death, her refusal to return the diamonds to the jewelers to whose care they were customarily entrusted is predicated on her understanding that to do so is to return them to "the estate": she may never be able to claim them again once she hands them over.

The ensuing complications are manifold: first, no one believes that Florian intended to give them to her as a personal gift, as Lizzie claims; even the less-than-perspicacious Lord Fawn recognizes that "such a necklace is not given by a husband even to a bride in the manner described by Lizzie" (I.92). Second, although the Eustace family believes "the plunder for the sake of tranquillity should be allowed" and is willing to let the matter drop on the assumption that the diamonds will eventually end up with Lizzie's son (the undisputed heir), their family lawyer, Mr. Camperdown, refuses to do so. His personal animosity toward Lizzie—he repeatedly calls her a "harpy" and refers to her (in)action as "robbery" and "stealing" (I.37)—propels a campaign that contributes to Lizzie's ruin at least as much as does her own willfulness. Her adamant insistence on keeping the useless diamonds, despite her knowledge that, as her aunt tells her, "You can't sell them—and as a widow you can't wear 'em" (I.52), registers as perverse in the novel's value system. Such is the contradictory status of a commodity that is supposed to be valued for its aesthetic qualities in enhancing the beauty of women, but is in fact primarily desired by men, either for its monetary value or for the status it confers on the owner.

Lizzie herself seems unclear as to why she wants to retain the gems; but as Nancy Armstrong has argued, the Victorian ideology of private life, of which the domestic novel is both a purveyor and a symptom, hinged on women's power as moral agents and their manipulation of signs and symbols *within* the household.[41] The manipulation of, or even excessive interest in, commodities and capital was antithetical to acceptable comportment, and the diamonds occupy a hazy middle ground between being women's things and family wealth. Mr. Camperdown reflects that "the widows with whom he had been called upon to deal, had been ladies quite content to accept the good things settled upon them by the liberal prudence of their friends and husbands—not greedy, bloodsucking harpies such as this Lady Eustace" (I.254), despite his concession that such "ladies" typically "filch china" (I.40) and silver from their husbands' estates. Women, it seems, may be at once greedy or deceitful and utterly respectable—Lady Hittaway spreads lies about Lizzie and Frank (II.170), Lady Fawn and Mrs. Graystock both covet wealthy daughters-in-law, and Lady Linlithgow cheats at cards (I.5)—as long as they practice within their proper sphere of influence. Lizzie, a woman possessed of "courage . . . power of language, and . . . force" (I.290), who "knew much" of "things to be learned by reading," having "really taken diligent trouble with herself" (I.18), deals freely with pawnbrokers, borrows money from disreputable jewelers in order to attract a wealthy man, and eventually even attempts to sell the Eustace diamonds. As Priscilla Walton has argued, Lizzie, rather than acting in relation to the men who would claim her, "acts *as* the man in trying to forge a subject position."[42] Unlike her grandfather-in-law, who sold family jewels with impunity, and unlike her cousin Frank, who steals a horse and is only lauded for riding it so well, Lizzie is harshly condemned as much for her bold economic transgressions involving gemstones as for her "grasping" nature.[43] D. A. Miller has observed that in the novels of Jane Austen, jewelry circulates "ubiquitously," but it "does so under two quite limited conditions: it must always have been *given* to the wearer, and given *only* by a relative or lover, in token of union through marriage or common blood."[44] While Lizzie's necklace would seem to map onto this model neatly, the outrage at her desire to keep it after her husband's death is fueled in large part by the commonly held sentiment that he ought not to have married her in the first place. It is bad enough that Lizzie Greystock manages to keep the Eustace name and the Eustace home; the idea of a woman who is clearly "dying to handle her money" (I.12) keeping the Eustace diamonds is a final outrage. Mr. Dove's ruling on heirlooms, which appears to favor Lizzie to some degree, has no effect on Camperdown's behavior; his moral certainty that Lizzie is unfit to be a Eustace trumps the law itself.

Yet in a novel that has typically been read as a social satire, the diamonds themselves are generally seen as little more than a plot device, the occasion not so much for crime as for revelation of character. A. O. J. Cockshut summarizes this point of view.

> The diamonds have two functions in the plot. They are the still centre round which all the characters and events are gathered. They are the point without magnitude which alone permits the ample circle of the story to be drawn. Every character is related to the diamond in a different way. For Mr. Camperdown they are in the wrong hands, and so are an emblem of an outrage upon justice. They appeal both to the obstinacy and the avarice of Lady Eustace. To Lord Fawn they are a possible stain upon his honour, if he marries the woman who is perhaps retaining them illegally. Frank Greystock sees them as a symbol of the persecution his cousin has to endure. For the Duke of Omnium they are the cause of an enjoyable scandal and for Lady Glencora a godsend for relieving the boredom of his invalid old age.[45]

All this is true enough, although for Camperdown the diamonds are primarily an emblem of his clients' wealth and social status, both of which he has personal and financial reasons (as well as his often-stated professional and ethical reasons) to uphold at all costs. Furthermore, different adamantine characteristics are used to describe various characters: thus Lucy Morris is a "treasure" (I.22, 23, 165) whose bright eyes seem to glisten like diamonds (I.24, 177); her sterling qualities are as "firm rocks" to her betrothed, Frank Greystock. He considers her to be "real stone" and his cousin Lizzie mere "paste" (II.230). The law firm of Camperdown and Son and the jewelers, Messrs. Garnett, are also "firm as rocks" (I.42), whereas Lord George's face is as "hard . . . as a rock" (II.327) when he takes leave of Lizzie. Lady Fawn, "in whose bosom there was no stony corner" (I.67), can neither give up Lucy nor blame Frank for neglecting her. The attractive but socially objectionable Mrs. Carbuncle's name puns on two current meanings of the term, a red gemstone and a malignant or infected growth. Lizzie herself is only diamondlike in that she is "hard."

Structurally, Lizzie's fate is intimately connected with her diamonds; they come and go from her life along with various male authority figures. Her father's death forces her to pawn the diamonds she has purchased for herself, her husband's death precipitates the Eustace diamond crisis, and her betrothal to Lord Fawn turns on her willingness to give up the necklace. Figured as a paste diamond whose "metal did not ring true" (I.21), Lizzie is played satirically against the early modern troping of virtuous women as diamonds. Trollope's allusions to Shakespeare are, as W. J. Mc-Cormack argues, prominent and wide-ranging.[46] McCormack also notes that Lizzie's unsuccessful attempts to engross herself in Spenser's *Faerie Queene* are "ironic, in that Spenser's Lady Una does indeed possess both unsullied purity and a true and faithful knight, whereas Lizzie lacks both" (389). The irony is furthered by the fact that in *The Faerie Queene,* the true and faithful Arthur's marvelous shield, made of one solid piece of flawless diamond, is a symbol of his knightly qualities. Trollope repeatedly contrasts Frank Greystock, caught between his loyalty to Lucy and his desire for Lizzie and "falling lamentably short in his heroism" (I.320), with "a hero—a man absolutely stainless, perfect as an Arthur—a man honest in all his dealings, equal to all trials, true in all his speech . . . and, above all, faithful in love" (I.318). And unlike the Faerie Queene who is the object of Arthur's quest, Lizzie in Frank's company is believed by her own servant to behave no better than a "quean at a fair" (I.218, 221). Although *quean* in this context could simply mean "common sort of young woman," it also carries the connotation of "prostitute." To call Lizzie a prostitute, however, would be to ignore the fact that in her dealings with men, she generally holds the purse strings; Trollope makes clear that whatever Lizzie's other attractions, her suitors are, to a man, after her money.

More recently, critics have paid attention to the metonymy between Lizzie's sexuality and both her diamonds and the iron box in which she keeps them. For William Cohen, "jewels" signifies "genitals" in a fairly straightforward Freudian manner.[47] Walton agrees that the increasingly hysterical attempts of male characters either to lock up or get hold of Lizzie's diamonds must be read as attempts to control her sexuality. Rather than being diamondlike in her purity, Lizzie shares with her gemstones their status as not-quite commodities, family possessions that may or may not be traded on the open market. Now that she is rich as well as beautiful, Lizzie is considered by her male relatives to be in a "period of danger" (I.14) as long as she is a free economic and sexual agent; the men agree among themselves that she must be married in order to be "placed under some decent control" (II.247).

The diamonds themselves, then, function as an organizing principle as well as a prominent symbolic motif. But they serve a less obvious structural purpose as well: the dispute over who does and, perhaps more tellingly, who should own them is doubled in a shadow story of colonial property claims. This claim concerns the fictional Sawab of Mygawb, whose case involves Lord Fawn both as a "Peer of Parliament and an Under-Secretary of State" for Indian Affairs (I.24); neither body can decide "whether the Sawab of Mygawb should have twenty millions of rupees paid to him and [be] placed upon a throne, or whether he should be kept in prison all his life" (I.25). Lucy, Lord Fawn's confidante, "mastered the subject, and almost got Lord Fawn into a difficulty by persuading him to stand up against his chief on behalf of the injured prince" (I.25). She argues that the Sawab "is being deprived of his own property—that he is kept out of his rights" (I.65). The property claim moves the plot forward by providing an occasion for the Tory member Frank Greystock to take up the Sawab's cause and publicly abuse Fawn for failing to do so, thus simultaneously mirroring his defense of Lizzie and driving another wedge between the two men. Other than that, the Sawab fades out of the story and tends to be overlooked by critics; even as John Halperin argues for *The Eustace Diamonds*'s place as a political novel, he writes that "the importance the Eustace controversy assumes in the political world is a direct commentary on the absurdity of the other ersatz issues of the day (such as the Sawab)." He calls the House of Commons debate over the Sawab "silly" even as he documents for us Trollope's profound absorption in real-life parliamentary politics and reminds us that Trollope ran unsuccessfully for Parliament himself in 1868.[48] Halperin, an acute critic of Trollope, is surely correct in characterizing the novel's tone as regards the Sawab—Trollope does treat the matter lightly—but actual Indian land-claim cases were intensely fought battles with profound consequences for Indian sovereigns and colonial administrators, if not for members of Parliament.

McCormack, too, in his notes to the Oxford edition, registers the novel's contemptuous treatment of the Sawab; he glosses the name by pointing out that "both the title and the place-name are of course invented, the first perhaps modelled on 'nabob' or 'nawab' and the second on 'Mysore'—such invented terms underline the dismissive attitude toward the prince whose complaint forms part of the dispute between Lord Fawn and Frank Greystock" (379–80). Although he argues that the novel has a colonial context, he sees that context in terms of parallel claims of robbery: "The Sawab has been robbed, or at least made a claim to that effect. The Eustaces claim that Lizzie has robbed them" (xxiv). I would frame the case somewhat differently and draw the parallel between Lizzie and the Sawab as claimants whose cases hinge on extralegal hegemonic notions of their unfitness to possess the power that their contested property would confer on them.

The Sawab's case bears a resemblance to a land claim that took place in 1862,[49] pressed by the maharajah (or rajah) of Mysore, Krishnaraja Odeya Wodeyar III.[50] The rajah of Mysore's case is worth examining, first, to balance (and complement) the critical attention that has been paid to possible real-life precedents to the Eustace case,[51] but also because it speaks to the workings of power in precisely the social and political milieu that Trollope was fictionalizing. Both the true and fictional property cases speak to the question of who is socially, as well as legally, entitled to inherit and possess property.

The rajah of Mysore was the heir of a Hindu royal family called the Halerys in the territory known to the British as Mysore; their unbroken rule has been traced by some historians back to 1664, although the history of ruling families in the region is fairly complex and cannot be plotted along a single dynastic axis. The Halerys and the family of the Muslim ruler Hyder Ali spent the last quarter of the eighteenth century in a shifting pattern of tentative alliances and conflict, but Hyder Ali and his more famous son Tipu Sultan devoted much energy to fighting the British encroachment into their territories; the Hindu Halerys, who had lost much of their territory to Hyder Ali, moved toward an alliance with the British, who saw them as a far lesser threat than Tipu. (Tipu had been specially targeted as an enemy by Governor-General Cornwallis, ostensibly for having aligned himself with the French.) In 1799, the fourth Anglo-Mysore war broke out between the East India Company and Tipu, and Mysore was taken by the British.[52] Here, then, is the first link that connects *The Eustace Diamonds* and *The Moonstone:* it was at the siege of Srirangapatna that Tipu's palace was stormed, Tipu was killed and his palace looted and, in Collins's novel, the Moonstone was stolen. The date that Collins's diamond enters the Herncastle family thus coincides with the purchase of the Eustace diamonds and their inscription into that family's record. This is also the date that the rajah of Mysore, the type for the Sawab of Mygawb, was restored to the possession of territories that eventually formed the basis of the 1862 dispute.

After General Baird took Srirangapatna, the Partition Treaty of

Mysore was drawn up and signed, giving various pieces of territory to the Nizam of Hyderabad and claiming for the British "Canara on the West, Wynad on the south-east; the districts of Darapuram and Coimbature and the town and island of Srirangapatna. . . . This settlement of Mysore as effected by Lord Wellesley, secured for the Company various substantial benefits, extended its territory from sea to sea across the base of the peninsula and later saw to the encircling of the Mysore kingdom by Pax Britannica."[53] The five-year-old Krishnaraja was given what was left of the kingdom and placed on the throne, and a British Resident was appointed to rule until he was of age. The Subsidiary Treaty of Seringapatam, signed July 8, 1799, also the work of Lord Wellesley, stipulated that the rajah was to pay the Company an annual subsidy of seven lakhs of star pagodas[54] in return for their maintaining a military force, and was to enter into no correspondence with any foreign state and to admit no foreign visitors without the knowledge and sanction of the Company.[55] It further stipulated that the British could assume control of Mysore simply by alleging misrule of any kind on the part of the rajah.

The rajah took the throne in 1812 and ruled until 1831, when a rebellion in Mysore was put down by British armed forces. Although British documents consistently refer to this uprising as a popular reaction against the rajah's misrule, its true causes and dimensions are difficult to ascertain from English sources. It is at least clear that peasants were rebelling in part against both the amount of taxes paid and the methods used to collect them, and that the British had been pressuring the rajah for some time to increase the level of tax revenue he paid to them. Having crushed the rebellion, the governor-general of India, Lord William Bentinck, citing the rajah's "gross misgovernment," ordered the administration of Mysore placed under the commissionership of Sir Mark Cubbon, a lieutenant-colonel in the Madras Infantry who had come to Madras as a cadet in 1800 and had attained the level of commissary-general for the Madras presidency.[56] The rajah was given a palace and a pension, and effectively stripped of power.

This arrangement persisted for almost thirty years, until Cubbon, in ill health, resigned his post in February 1861 (he died that April at Suez on his way home to England and was thus unable to give an opinion on the dispute that followed his resignation). On hearing that Cubbon planned to retire, the rajah wrote to the governor-general of India,

Charles Canning, requesting that he be reinstated as ruler of Mysore. His petition begins with a recapitulation of the history of Mysore since 1799.

> In the year 1799 the all-powerful English nation conquered the armies of Tippoo, stormed the fortress of Seringapatam, and slew the usurper, and then that great statesman, Lord Wellesley, founded a noble and disinterested policy, which added immensely to the fame of the British Government. . . . The Governor General waived all right of conquest, rescued me, then an infant, the rightful heir to the throne of Mysore, and the descendant of a long line of kings, from captivity, and restored me to the musnud of my ancestors. By an article in the treaty between the British Government and myself, it was provided that, if at any time the affairs of my country fell into confusion, the British Government should have the power of assuming management of the country until order was restored.[57]

The rajah's petition asserts that he has been uniformly loyal to England over the past half-century, and that when the government intervened to remove him from power, he did not resist. He further asserts (correctly) that Bentinck subsequently altered his opinion and favored returning the rajah to the throne, and that now, since Mark Cubbon so effectively put in place a "native system of government" that needs no modification, his restoration to the throne should be effected.

> And here I hope I may be pardoned, if I express my individual opinion, as one of the Sovereigns of India, on your Lordship's just and wise treatment of the native princes of this great country, in strengthening their hands, elevating their position, and consolidating their possessions. A day will come, my Lord . . . when these princes and chiefs, bound to your Government by a double tie of gratitude and self-interest, will present a bulwark which neither the wave of foreign invasion nor the tide of internal disaffection can throw down. . . . [In granting my petition] you will add another jewel to that immortal crown which your Lordship has earned by your generous advocacy and support of the princes of India.[58]

The strategies of appeal in this document are powerful—the rajah at once stakes his claim based on a legal and hereditary right to kingship that must necessarily resonate with the English and couches demand, flattery, and veiled threat in the rhetoric of the King James Bible, thus writing himself into being as a British subject even as he places himself in opposition to those in power. He raises what was in 1861 an all-too-familiar specter of revolt and foreign invasion, possibly in concert with one another, but claims that justice done will avert another rebellion as well as "add another jewel to that immortal crown" that will someday be Canning's reward, as in the Second Epistle of Peter, in which Peter writes that the reward of the righteous is a "crown of glory that does not fade away" (1 Pet. 5:4). The actual figure of the jewel in the crown is taken from Zechariah and suggests salvation both temporal and eternal ("on that day the Lord their God will save them for they are the flock of his people; for like the jewels of a crown they shall shine on his land" [Zech. 9:16]).[59]

At this time, of course, India had long been known as the "jewel in the crown" of the British Empire. The rajah thus wrenches the phrase out of its place as a metaphor for territory that he considers to be partly his and resettles it squarely back in a biblical context in which crowns are heavenly rewards for the righteous, not earthly ones for the rapacious. Bernard Cohn has written that "Kings in the medieval Hindu tradition were the controllers of the earth and its products, and in cosmographic terms jewels were the essence of the earth, its most pure and concentrated substance" (319).[60] The rajah's reframing of the metaphor of the jewel in the crown roundly rejects both the synecdochic troping of India as a jewel and the British right to retain it.

Over a year later, Canning sent a reply summarily dismissing the claim as "mistaken and untenable" (Parliamentary Papers, 4). Canning addresses a line in the original claim in which the rajah acknowledges, "I never hesitate to assert that the present enviable state of Mysore is attributable to the enlightened services of Sir Mark Cubbon, whose acknowledgements of my support have received your Lordship's recognition." Clearly in this context, the "support" of which the rajah speaks is synonymous with the "loyalty" he has shown to Cubbon and is a veiled reference to the fact that during the Rebellion of 1857, the rajah had sided with the British. Canning, however, pounces on this sentence and attacks.

> Your Highness . . . after a candid avowal that the present enviable state of Mysore is attributable to the enlightened services of Sir M. Cubbon, has referred to a supposed recognition by me, not only of the loyalty displayed by your Highness [during the events of 1857] but also of support given by your Highness to that officer during his long and able administration. Had Sir Mark Cubbon ever acknowledged such support, your

Highness must feel sure that nothing would have been more agreeable to me than to have had it in my power, on such good grounds, to attribute to your Highness a share in the credit due for the successful administration of Mysore. . . . I cannot conceal from your Highness that throughout the correspondence between Sir M. Cubbon and this Government, extending as it does over so many years, I have failed to find any such acknowledgement. Sir Mark Cubbon has left on record opinions of an entirely contrary character. (5)

Canning argues that Wellesley, far from waiving any right of conquest when he placed the child on the throne, "asserted and maintained that right in all its integrity" (5). First, Wellesley's drafting of the partition treaty constituted his chief assertion of the right of conquest, and the rajah was not party to the treaty except "as the notified future recipient of the liberality of the British Government" (5). Second, the fact that the British government made over to the rajah land taken from Tipu that the rajah's ancestors had never ruled "was based distinctly upon the British Government's right of conquest" (5), and in fact the rajah had no inherited patrimony to claim. Canning later elaborates on this assertion by stating that whatever provision has been made for the rajah through the good offices of England is "a personal right, not an heritable one. It is not claimable as a right even by a natural-born heir" (5).[61] In other words, not only do the rajah's descendants have no claim on the throne, they cannot even claim the income he currently enjoys. Finally, Canning claims that the subsidiary treaty's stipulation regarding the British Government's right to assume the rule of Mysore demonstrated that "far from waiving the rights derived from conquest, Lord Wellesley, in a very signal manner, kept those rights alive" (5). Therefore, he reasons, in asking for a restoration that was neither implied nor promised, the rajah, who for the twenty years of his rule "flagrantly and habitually violated" the terms of his accession despite "repeated warnings and remonstrances," now "challenges the justice and good faith of the British Government." Canning asserts that England has assumed a sacred and inviolate moral responsibility to the people of Mysore whom it rescued from the rajah in 1831, and that "if the authority of the British officers were removed, or even hampered, the peace and prosperity of Mysore would be at an end" (4–7).

Thus rebuffed, the rajah, like Trollope's fictional Sawab, appealed to

the Home authorities in the person of Sir Charles Wood, the Secretary of
State for India. Meeting Canning on his own terms, the rajah gives an al-
ternate reading of the post-1799 history in which he demonstrates, using
Wellesley's letters, that the arrangements in Mysore were neither indul-
gences nor recognitions of moral obligations but were designed to "'se-
cure the Company a less invidious and more efficient share of revenue,
resource, commercial advantage and military strength than could be obtained under any other distribution of territory or power'" (8).

Wood responded with a lengthy letter in which he rejected the appeal
and denied the possibility of the rajah's establishing "any right to be restored to his former position" (16). There were, however, dissenters to this
opinion. Three members of the Council of India—Sir Henry Montgomery, a longtime official of the Madras government; Sir Frederic Currie, the former chairman of the East India Company and the man who ne-
gotiated the Treaty of Amritsar at the end of the first Anglo-Sikh war; and
Sir John Willoughby—each wrote separate opinions supporting the rajah's claim. Montgomery demonstrated that Lord William Bentinck, the
man who removed the rajah from power, had by 1833 come to believe that
"the derangement of the affairs of Mysore under the rajah's rule had been
greatly exaggerated" (19), and his removal was both unnecessary and un-
justified under the terms of the Subsidiary Treaty. Currie declared Canning's decision to be "impolitic as well as unjust" (25). All three dissenters
objected to Canning's tone as well as to his reading of history. These opinions, however, did not indicate an anti-imperialist viewpoint or a desire
for Indian self-rule. Rather, these were men committed to the imperialist
project, and as such they knew the value of honoring treaties and of ced-
ing limited power to the so-called princely states[62] as means of maintaining rather than giving up control. Their protests, however, had no effect.

Defeated, the rajah attempted a final strategy: he requested permission to adopt a son to inherit the rule of Mysore. While both the governor-general and the Home Office wished to refuse the rajah this request,
once again the dissenting opinions reveal what was at stake. When he began his attempt to regain the throne, the rajah assumed that at sixty-
seven he would not live many years longer; having been denied his
restoration, and having survived both of his sons, his next move was to
petition to be allowed to adopt a child. Under a relatively new British
policy known as the Doctrine of Lapse, put in place by Governor-General Dalhousie, if the rajah died lacking an heir, Mysore, now a princely

state in name only, would cease to be a princely state altogether and would become a piece of British territory outright. This doctrine also forbade princes to adopt heirs, an established practice in much of India, and it was on this basis that the rajah's final request was denied. One dissenting India Board member argued that the no-adoption clause in particular was "novel and unjust, [and] opposed to all custom and religions in India" (71); Currie's dissent attributed the 1857 Revolt in large part to Indian outrage over the subsumation of the princely states of "Sattara . . . Kerowlee, Nagpore, Jhansee, &tc." (46) under this rule.

Permitted to adopt a child only as his personal heir, the rajah did so. He died in 1868, and it was not until well after his death (and the publication of *The Eustace Diamonds*) that Parliament agreed to make his adopted son and personal heir the heir to the throne of Mysore as well when he came of age in 1881.

In portraying MPs who approach Indian claims with a combination of ignorance and disdain, Trollope thus is acting as a faithful recorder of the political milieu with which he was intimately acquainted. Furthermore, although we never hear the Sawab's side, we have reasons to mistrust those who will determine his fate: clearly, Fawn is a fool and Greystock an opportunist, and neither cares about the Sawab except as it affects his career. But what Trollope knew such claims to be about—property as power and as means to generate political and social capital as well as a source of enormous wealth in itself—could not be more relevant to the novel's political context, which is to say its colonial context.

So in *The Eustace Diamonds*'s parallel property dispute, Lizzie's diamonds, which represent the title of which she is deemed unworthy as well as those aspects of her self that need to be brought under "decent control," synecdochically double the Indian soil out of which they were mined. As Lizzie fights to keep Indian diamonds which may or may not be hers legally, the Sawab, in asking to be placed back on his throne, is fighting to keep Indian territory from being annexed by the British. As in the figure of the jewel in the crown, land and the wealth it represents is troped as a diamond, and vice versa. This troublesome conflation of women and diamonds, territory and sexuality, property and plunder, introduced in *The Surgeon's Daughter* and played out so explicitly in *The Moonstone,* returns in another guise in *The Eustace Diamonds* and again demonstrates the ways in which the language of fiction constructed the idea and the reality of India, abroad and at home.

CHAPTER FOUR

Tea and the Mode of (Literary) Production

That an Oriental drink could hold an entire nation in its thrall is one of the strangest quirks of social history.
—Arup Kumar Dutta, *Cha Garam! The Tea Story*

It is possible that tea is at least mentioned in every canonical mid-Victorian novel. If tea the drink is thought of today as the English national beverage, and tea the meal as a quintessentially English habit, these developments are largely due to tea's rise in popularity in the nineteenth century. Tea often took tortuous paths on its way into English households and English novels; different moments in its life cycle are variously celebrated and ignored as it moves from being a Chinese cash crop to an Indian colonial enterprise to the emblem of middle-class English domesticity. Tea's often violent nineteenth-century history intersects with the English opium trade and British wars with China and Burma that led to the annexation and "opening" of Assam. Yet once tea enters the domicile, where it is surrounded by the treasured accoutrements of its storage, preparation, and disposal rituals, it is magically reinvented as that which makes home homelike.

Tea was never fully domesticated in the sense that its origins were absolutely forgotten, but the odd status it attained in the nineteenth century as what Roland Barthes has called England's "totem-drink"[1] suggests a kind of hyperdisplacement. The Victorians certainly knew that tea came from Asia, but as Marx wrote, they "look no further than the grocer's [when] they buy their tea."[2] If commodity fetishism is the result of the processes whereby the "social characteristics of men's own labour" come to be understood as "objective characteristics of the products of labour themselves,"[3] then as an imported commodity tea was, for its English consumers, dislodged from its place of origin and original producers as well as from the English merchants who brought it to the domestic marketplace. As Anne McClintock has argued, "The domestic realm, far from being the antithesis of industrial rationality, is revealed to be entirely structured by commodity fetishism,"[4] and tea's place in the novel is always overdetermined, freighted with symbolism of home and family, security and comfort and respectability—in short, domesticity—so as to shut out any suggestion of the intertwined strands of private industry, government policy, and military intervention necessary to bring it to the table. Even in one notable counterexample—the brief moment in *Cranford* when the aged Miss Matty, her savings lost, turns to selling tea out of her home to pay her bills—she does so because tea is so respectable and so thoroughly gendered as to be hardly a commodity, and the selling of it barely a business.[5] "Consumption" is a multivalent term, and consumers may be said to consume tea twice: when they buy it and when they drink it. Having Matty preside over quaint tea-measuring rituals in her home collapses one sense of the word into the other; her tea selling becomes another form of tea party. When Matty is relieved of her commercial duties by the return of her long-lost brother from India, the role of sustaining the family through the fruits of colonial enterprise is regendered male, much to everyone's relief.

Representations of tea drinking in Victorian novels tend to suggest comfort rather than elegance, and they carry little trace of the suggestions of unearned luxury and possible dire physical, psychological, and social effects that hovered around eighteenth-century discussions of tea (although Matty's suspicion of green tea, which she attempts to dissuade her customers from buying, is one of Gaskell's many jokes about Cranford's backwardness). Victorian tea drinking is a middle-of-the-road pleasure, much like novel reading itself. This domestication of the tea table, the persistent impulse to locate "tea" always and only inside the English home, and to think of it as something belonging in some peculiarly emblematic way to English culture, serves to occlude questions of origins and of economics at the very moment at which English planters were beginning to cultivate tea for the first time ever in India.[6] Some Indians drank tea before the mid-nineteenth century, but they did not grow it, and English tea drinkers who had become connoisseurs of Chinese tea, much of which was green tea, were forced to switch their allegiance to a new product—Indian black tea.[7]

James Walvin has observed that by the end of the eighteenth century, when the habit of tea drinking had trickled down from royalty and nobility to the rest of the nation, it effected "a subtle change in the way millions of people behaved. British sociability itself had changed, revolving, at certain key times of the day and for particular occasions, around the serving of tea. Tea insinuated itself into every walk of life."[8] By the mid-nineteenth century, tea drinking had become a socially and morally important activity across the social spectrum, and the making of tea a ritual over which women generally presided. An 1853 article in *Fraser's Magazine* titled "Indian Teas and Chinese Travellers" asks, "Is there an occasion upon which our fair countrywomen better display their graceful affability and delicacy of hand and wrist than when, with the 'fluttering urn' before them . . . they dispense the delicious brewage?"[9] In this image, the making and serving of tea allows women to perform and to display themselves in a socially appropriate manner, just as they do when playing music for company; women who preside at the tea table are performing, but they are performing simultaneously the fact of their "affability" (willingness to please) and their "delicacy." The very tautology of the way in which tea and women are thus linked is no small part of its appeal: good women make tea; making tea makes you good. But prior to the nineteenth century, tea's reputation in English culture was hardly benign.

Tea was unknown to the English before the mid-seventeenth century, but Marx refers to it, not without irony, as an "indispensable" beverage.[10] Its rise to prominence was, however, as Dutta points out, neither natural nor inevitable.[11] Tea appeared in England along with its rivals coffee and chocolate, and it was available only to city dwellers who purchased leaves from the new establishments known as coffeehouses (not teahouses, because coffee was initially more popular).[12] Catherine, wife of Charles II, introduced tea to the English court, and the East India Company placed the first specific order for tea in 1664, but importation was sporadic until the East India Company began trading directly with China in 1700, an arrangement that was to last until 1836. Tea continued to be consumed at court under William and Mary and then Anne, usually in the evening, but it was highly taxed and costly. It was not until the 1760s and beyond that smugglers began their highly organized and widespread trade; prices of smuggled tea were low enough to make it available to common people throughout England.[13]

By making available a steady supply at affordable prices, smugglers paradoxically brought a certain stability to the market, thus making it possible for tea to gain a foothold in English culture. Tea began to convey something about personal identity later in the eighteenth century, when it was championed by both Samuel Johnson and the temperance movement, and famously praised by William Cowper in "The Task" as "the cups / That cheer but not inebriate."[14] But tea and Englishness did not become inextricably entwined until around the time when British merchants took hold of the means of production and began to grow and manufacture tea rather than merely trading in it. Although it was not until 1887 that the consumption of Indian black tea matched that of Chinese tea,[15] and it was not until the end of the nineteenth century that it dominated the trade, the *idea* of tea grown in India by the English gained currency before the enterprise itself had stabilized.

Despite its growing popularity in the eighteenth century, tea's association with both the vice of luxury and the crime of smuggling kept its reputation volatile. John Galt's 1821 novel *Annals of the Parish,* set in a country parish in Scotland between the years 1760 and 1810, adeptly traces shifts in the way tea's social role was understood. In chapter 2, "Year 1761," the narrator Micah Balwhidder notes, "It was in this year that the great smuggling trade corrupted all the west coast. . . . The tea was going like the chaff, the brandy like well-water."[16] Like the eighteenth-century pamphleteers, Balwhidder repeatedly equates the evils of tea with those of alcohol. The year 1761 brings a host of plagues to the parish of Dalmailing, including the widespread drinking of brandy and the unlooked-for arrival of "three contested bastard bairns" and a dancing master. Tea is not least among these.

> Before this year, the drinking of tea was little known in the parish, saving among a few of the heritors' houses on a Sabbath evening, but now it became very rife, yet the commoner sort did not like to let it be known that they were taking to the new luxury, especially the elderly women, who, for that reason, had their ploys in outhouses and byplaces, just as the witches lang syne had their sinful possets and galravitchings. . . . Well do I remember one night in harvest, in this very year . . . that I heard [Thomas Thorl's] wife, and two three other carlins, with their bohea in the inside of the hedge, and no doubt but it had a lacing of the conek

[cognac], for they were all cracking like pen-guns. But I gave them a sign by a loud host, that Providence sees all, and . . . I heard them, like guilty creatures, whispering and gathering up their truck-pots and trenchers, and cowering away home.[17]

The very next year, however, Balwhidder's wife encourages a local widow to supplement her income by selling tea, and he is forced to concede that tea drinking is less harmful than alcohol consumption and stops preaching against it. By 1781, Balwhidder mentions visitors to his home drinking tea without feeling the need to justify further,[18] although he still inveighs against smuggling. From the vantage point of 1821, Balwhidder's moral panic and its dissipation are clearly meant to be comical; throughout the novel, Galt's humor is inherently self-congratulatory, implicitly positioned as it is from the standpoint of the "modern" author (and readers) who accept as normal that which their forefathers found alien and threatening. The twenty-year process of tea's domestication and normalization he outlines, however, maps closely onto Beth Kowaleski-Wallace's argument that complaints about the "'pernicious' habit of tea-drinking"[19] among the lower classes peaked in the mid-eighteenth century. Tea drinking was equated with the consumption of gin and was thought to weaken the social fabric by facilitating gossip, scandal, and idleness, and to encourage women in particular to waste time and money.[20] Its pernicious effect on the human body was regularly asserted. A typical example, Annabella Plumptre's 1810 *Domestic Management; or, The Healthful Cookery-Book,* recapitulated mid-eighteenth century advice in its warning against tea.

> The frequent drinking of a quantity of tea, as is the general practice, relaxes and weakens the tone of the stomach, whence proceeds nausea and indigestion, with a weakness of the nerves, and flabbiness of the flesh, and very often a pale wan complexion.[21]

Tea, she continues, should be avoided by persons with weak nerves, and "green tea is less wholesome than black."[22] In *Sanditon* (1817), Jane Austen satirizes this view by having the hypochondriacal Arthur Parker, a devotee of wine and hot chocolate, lecture Charlotte on the sinister nature of green tea, of which she has dared to take two cups: "What Nerves you must have. . . . It acts on me like Poison and wd [*sic*] entirely take away the use of my right side, before I had swallowed it 5 minutes."[23]

The ill effects of green tea would, however, seem to have been a dead issue by the mid-nineteenth century. In her influential 1861 *Book of Household Management,* Mrs. Beeton repeats Florence Nightingale's injunction against giving too much tea to invalids (advice that, to judge by the novels, was widely ignored) but otherwise leaves the subject alone.[24] Tea's place in the homes of the middle and lower classes was no longer controversial, and relatively little attention was paid specifically to green tea.[25] There is no one moment at which the medical and moral opposition to tea dissolved, but with the reduction of the import tax on tea from 199 percent to 12.5 percent in 1784, tea ceased to be a luxury item,[26] and the eighteenth-century clamor against tea, which was in part driven by irritation that the poor were appropriating a habit of the wealthy,[27] gradually died down. By 1852, annual consumption of tea had reached almost 54 million pounds, and by 1860 was up to nearly 76 million.[28] By this time, however, the commodity known as tea was beginning to be something other than what it had been previously.

As long as the lucrative China trade remained untroubled, officials of the East India Company failed to act on suggestions, tendered as early as the 1770s, that tea cultivation be attempted in India. Yet historians have argued persuasively that the discovery of indigenous tea plants in Assam was a significant factor in the East India Company's decision to annex it in 1826. The Ahom people who lived in Assam had been skirmishing periodically with the Burmese since 1817, and Company officials in Bengal claimed to feel sufficiently threatened by 1824 to declare war on the Burmese on their own behalf and eventually to seize Assam outright in a series of maneuvers that, in their contradiction of company policy, generated considerable internal controversy.[29] Meanwhile, in 1836 the East India Company lost its monopoly on the China trade (that is, its role as sole purchaser of Chinese teas for England), and the search for new sources of tea began in earnest. At the same time, Chinese dissatisfaction with the British refusal to pay for tea with anything but opium was reaching a breaking point.

The trade imbalance caused by England's purchase of vast quantities of tea from China (4.5 million tons annually by the mid-eighteenth century) had finally begun to be offset in the 1760s by the sale of opium, grown by the British in India (particularly Bengal), to China.[30] Although China made this trade illegal with laws passed in 1796 and 1800,[31] it continued largely unchecked until March 1839, when the Chinese forced the

British to deliver "20,283 chests of [English] opium" to be destroyed.[32] By the end of October, armed conflict was imminent, and the first military engagement took place on November 3, 1839.

The first Anglo-Chinese, or Opium, War (1840–42) slowed the tea trade with China at precisely the moment that British settlers were beginning to cultivate this same cash crop in India. Although wild tea plants grew in India, tea had never been cultivated there. But in 1838, in a classic example of Marxian primitive accumulation, hundred-acre grants of so-called waste lands or officially unoccupied territory in Assam were offered to planters with forty-five-year leases, contingent upon the cultivation of tea.[33] Although local people were not excluded in theory, the requirement that applicants possess three hundred rupees worth of capital or stock "excluded Indian competition in practice."[34] The Assam Company was formed in 1839, and a land rush began. Large-scale planting and the introduction of mechanized processes of rolling and drying the leaves, as well as the anxiety generated by periodic interruptions of the China trade, resulted in Indian black tea's movement into the English market by 1850. By 1859, forty-eight estates under British ownership were producing over a million pounds of tea annually,[35] laborers were being shipped in from all over India under highly questionable conditions, and the local economy of the Ahom, which had been largely based on the production of silk and cotton textiles, was radically transformed. Tea cultivation was taken up in Northwest India, along the southwestern coast, and in Sri Lanka.

The burgeoning South Asian tea industry and the related activities of speculation, investment, and shipping were frequently described in a wide range of periodicals. Such articles as "Cultivation of the Tea-Plant in Assam" (*Penny Magazine,* 1840), "The Tea-Plant" and "Culture of Tea in the Himalayan Mountains" (*Hogg's Weekly Instructor,* 1846, 1852), "Indian Teas and Chinese Travellers" (*Fraser's Magazine,* 1853), "Travel and Adventures in the Province of Assam" (*New Quarterly Review,* 1855), and "Making Tea in India" (*All The Year Round,* 1864) kept the possibilities of Indian tea before the public even when the tea itself was unavailable or of inferior quality. The tone of the articles tends to be optimistic; the 1840 article in Charles Knight's *Penny Magazine* rehearses what will become familiar arguments in favor of Indian tea cultivation—freedom from dependence on China, prosperity for British entrepreneurs, and the opportunity to expose Indian workers to the moral benefits of wage labor. The article begins, "For some years our intercourse [with China] has been in an uncertain and unsatisfactory state, and at this moment is totally suspended. . . . It is not however the suspension of the trade—for that may be only temporary—which gives importance to the subject of [tea cultivation], but its connection with the welfare and happiness of that mighty empire placed under our dominion in India."[36] The author gestures briefly at the fact that the "welfare and happiness" of Indian textile workers have been compromised by the introduction of British factory-made textiles into India's traditional external markets as well as India itself.

> The trial now making in Assam to cultivate the tea plant for commercial purposes derives its importance from the advantages which the introduction of a branch of industry suited to their quiet and sedentary habits will confer upon our fellow-subjects in India. They have been deprived of their occupations in many instances, and their skill and industry have been superseded by the power-looms of Manchester and Glasgow; but if we could be supplied with tea from India instead of China, such an employment as the cultivation and making of tea would promote peaceful habits of industry among the Hindoos, would render the slopes of barren mountains fruitful, and add an additional staple for export equal in value to that of the aggregate mass of indigenous articles now shipped to England, and thus prevent the loss in exchange which the East India Company experience in remitting home their territorial revenues.[37]

The perceived need to promote "peaceful habits of industry" among Indian workers, as well as the reference to Manchester, suggests that the writer (most likely Knight himself) is reading the situation in India through the lens of domestic developments, particularly that of various organized labor movements and bread or food riots, "repeated cases of which," E. P. Thompson notes, could "be found in almost every town and county until the 1840s."[38] In yoking together the handloom weavers of India and Manchester, Knight asks the English workers at once to make an imaginative connection between the two and to accept their own fate as future factory workers just as the Indians are presumed to accept their place in a radically different and possibly uncongenial métier.[39] In an analysis of *Penny Magazine,* Michael Feldberg has argued that this successful example of the so-called workingmen's journals cannot be considered apolitical despite its rigid editorial policy excluding discussions of politics, religion, and news of the day. Feldberg observes that *Penny Mag-*

azine "endlessly canted the values which the middle classes prescribed for those below them"; the readership "was enjoined to keep out of pubs, attend reading rooms and lectures, save its pennies, and live content in the fact of adversity."[40] He focuses on an image Knight uses of the worker coming home to his cheerful, singing teakettle, noting that Mayhew's poor were unlikely to notice the cheeriness of their kettles. The political nature of Knight's work may be seen clearly enough in the passage on tea cultivation: English workers, in being asked to endorse the passing on of a value they apparently already possess ("peaceful habits of industry"), thereby capitulate to the notion that they have indeed internalized it. Yet what is striking about this passage is its internationalization of the unemployed handloom weaver, a figure that haunts the industrial novels as a symbol of what England specifically has lost due to mechanization. This collapsing of Indian and English weavers is profoundly problematic in that it incorporates multiple classes of Indian workers "as only a contingent element in another history with another subject";[41] still, it gestures at a set of connections that are virtually never made directly in the industrial novels.[42] Yet English industrial workers are linked repeatedly with the idea of tea as a civilizing force.[43]

While Victorian journalists were eager to explain the business of tea to their readers, novels rarely speak of commerce and tea in the same register. If Indian workers could be improved by growing tea, English workers needed only to drink it. By the 1840s, the old associations of tea with scandal had virtually disappeared from English novels, and the socializing properties of the tea table were understood to have a salutary effect. Tea's presence on the tables of the working class in mid-Victorian novels indicates their possession of middle-class ideals of virtue and industry. The prejudice against working-class tea drinking endured at least through the 1820s, when William Cobbett recapitulated the threefold argument in *Cottage Economy*, directing it specifically toward factory workers and rural laborers: that tea drinking wasted time and money, undermined health, and eroded women's morals by promoting gossip and scandal *among the working class.*

> It must be evident to every one that the practice of tea drinking must render the frame feeble, and unfit to encounter hard labour. . . . Hence succeeds a softness, an effeminacy, a seeking for the fire side, a lurking in the bed. . . . The drinking of tea . . . corrupts boys as soon as they are able

to move from home, and does little less for the girls to whom the gossip of the tea table is no bad preparatory school for the brothel.[44]

Tea in this reading siphons off both male and female labor power and sends them to bed, albeit for different purposes. As absurd as his hyperbolic claims may appear from the vantage point of the twenty-first century, however, it should be noted that Cobbett's attack on tea is made in the context of a campaign to preserve what he perceived to be the dying practice of brewing and drinking ale rather than tea. It was a losing battle, in part because caffeine (which, although identified as such in 1819, was absent from public discussions of tea's properties in the popular literature of the Victorian period) was perhaps more suited to the new forms and practices of labor in the nineteenth century than was alcohol.[45] Certainly, Cobbett's vaguely nationalistic attacks on tea were rapidly becoming anachronisms. By the mid-Victorian period, mainstream novels tend to reinforce the perhaps equally ludicrous idea expressed in *Fraser's* in 1853 that tea strengthens rather than weakens the social fabric. Tea, it is claimed,

> has a levelling and equalizing spirit. . . . When we consider the proud natures of our countrymen, and how much they shrink from receiving a favour they cannot return, we perceive that some medium was requisite to their social existence, within the reach of all and despised by none, to put them upon a common footing. Dinner, as a means of intercourse, excellent as it was and is, was yet obviously not always available to the humbler classes of the English. Ale-bouts excluded the gentler sex. Tea, therefore, which every man can without expense offer to his neighbour . . . which the cottager can hand to the lady who shelters in her cottage without fear of shocking her refined taste; around which poor and rich can sit, and do sit, on terms of equality and fellowship—is pre-eminently and intrinsically suited to the exigencies of our social position.[46]

This clearly untenable fantasy of tea's ability to transcend boundaries of class and gender appears in the context of a narrative of the Scottish botanist Robert Fortune's travels in the 1840s to China to obtain tea plants to be cultivated in India, in defiance of Chinese law. "Indian Teas and Chinese Travellers" is primarily a celebration of England's imminent independence from China and the concomitant restoration of England's proper place in terms of international trade relations.

When, indeed, we reflect upon the terms on which we have hitherto con-
sented to accept commerce from the Chinese . . . and how little advance
we have made during that entire space of time, in the endeavour to place
our intercourse with them upon the same footing that our merchants
hold with other nations, this fact of the establishment and prosperous
working of tea-plantations in our own possessions becomes, for many
reasons, matter for the greatest congratulations.[47]

Thus the essay's early effusions over tea's salutary effects on British health
and sociability serve as preface to the real point: Indian tea is good for
British trade, the British economy, and British national pride.

The notion that tea might bring people of different classes together
seems borrowed from the industrial novels of the 1840s and is perhaps
most strikingly rehearsed in Disraeli's *Sybil,* published in 1845.[48] In book
2, Sybil Gerard, the self-proclaimed daughter of the people whose hereditary title and lands will be restored to her by the novel's end, goes on a
mission of mercy to the home of the displaced handloom-weaver
Warner. His wife is ill, his children starving. Sybil brings the family food,
fuel, and money, but the focus of attention is tea.

> "What have you there, Warner?" [said his wife]. "Is that tea? Oh! I should
> like some tea. I do think tea would do me some good. I have quite a long-
> ing for it." . . . Sybil and Warner re-entered; the fire was lit, the tea made,
> the meal partaken of. An air of comfort, even of enjoyment, was diffused
> over this chamber, but a few minutes back so desolate and unhappy.
>
>   "Well," said the wife, raising herself a little up in her bed, "I feel as if
> that dish of tea had saved my life. Amelia, have you had any tea? And
> Maria? You see what it is to be good, girls; the Lord will never desert you.
> The day is fast coming when that Harriet will know what the want of a
> dish of tea is, with all her fine wages."[49]

What in "Indian Teas and Chinese Travellers" is called "the republican nature of tea"[50] here asserts itself. Yet the connection across class boundaries
that it facilitates is manifestly denied by Sybil; she implicitly identifies herself with the Warners in asking them, "who should sympathise with the
poor, but the poor?"[51] The novel's answer to this question—"who should
sympathise with the poor?"—turns out precisely to be that the rich
should, and must, sympathize with the poor if the poor are to be turned
away from revolutionary violence. Throughout the novel, Sybil Gerard

aligns herself rhetorically with the poor but is always being marked as different from them: her hereditary claim to nobility, not her poverty or her status as a daughter of the people, is her defining characteristic and the paradoxical source of her will to help the workers. Unlike the families who have purchased titles whom I discuss in chapter 2, the Gerards embody the ideals of the old order that freely dispenses charity to those under the protection of the manor. *Sybil* thus reveals itself to be riven by a formal contradiction: it tells two intersecting stories, that of Sybil's restoration to her proper station in life and that of the failure of Chartism, in which the latter is a species of fortunate fall that allows the aristocracy to reclaim its duties as well as its privileges. The triumphal fetishizing of elite philanthropy thus depends structurally on the refusal to allow laborers a voice, despite the fact that Walter and Sybil Girard prove their worth precisely by championing the Chartist cause. The novel begins by giving us the figure of a worker, Walter Girard, who will lead the workers, and then systematically and decisively undermines the philosophical underpinnings of the self-determination of labor. Sybil's drinking tea with the Warners, figured as an act of identification and solidarity, is instead a crossing of class boundaries for philanthropic purposes.

Scenes in which the working poor drink tea among themselves have a different if related value. They frequently signal a moment of respite from the harsher aspects of life in which it is possible to capture fleetingly some of the order and abundance of middle-classness, as in the "Manchester tea party" described in Gaskell's 1848 novel *Mary Barton.*

> On [the table], resting against the wall, was a bright green japanned tea-tray, having a couple of scarlet lovers embracing in the middle. The fire-light danced merrily on this, and really (setting all taste but that of a child's aside) it gave a richness of colouring to that side of the room. It was in some measure propped up by a crimson tea-caddy, also of japan ware.[52]

And shortly thereafter:

> What an aspect of comfort did [John Barton's] house-place present, after [Alice's] humble cellar! She did not think of comparing; but for all that she felt the delicious glow of the fire, the bright light that revelled in every corner of the room, the savoury smells, the comfortable sounds of a boiling kettle, and the hissing, frizzling ham.[53]

In terms of style, this is Gaskell at her worst: the exclamation mark as well as the piling-on of descriptors (*bright, merrily, delicious, bright, savoury, comfortable, hissing, frizzling*) reduce the writing to the level of bathos, aided by what seems to be an assertion that the people most likely to be pleased by this ostensibly delightful tableau of working-class hominess are children. Furthermore, this scene of domestic comfort insists on its own completeness even as it repeatedly raises the specter of the marketplace: Mary has to purchase eggs, ham, milk, bread, and rum before the guests can be fed, and the party itself is ruined by Alice's ill-timed mention of Mrs. Barton's absent sister Esther, a prostitute. Structurally, the novel gives the lie to its own marking of this scene as a domestic norm: this is to be the last such family gathering before Mrs. Barton dies in childbirth. The power of such "social problem novels" as *Mary Barton* lies in their ability to engage readers in their scenes of suffering so effectively that they accept gratefully the means of relief offered. The fact that the means of relief are invariably home comforts has been critiqued in terms of a middle-class conservatism that refuses social solutions to social problems.[54] And when "the world" to which "the home" is opposed is expanded to mean the entire British Empire, the empire is figured as only a site of commerce, a world that exists in contradistinction to the British home but itself needs no home to come home to. If, in the novels' terms, handloom weavers or cotton-spinners in Manchester can at least go home to tea, the tea workers themselves simply fail to materialize. Labor abuses on the Assam plantations resulted in several widely publicized inquiries, but by this time, to associate tea with Englishness was to divorce it from any and all questions of its existence prior to its arrival in English shops. The novels thus succeed both in incorporating India and making its concerns irrelevant. The actual residents of Assam, most of whom did not work on the tea plantations, were invariably referred to in the press as "hill-tribes" and described, as in the *New Monthly Magazine* in 1847, as "fierce," "half-savage," and so forth.[55] But tea's power to socialize potentially fierce mill-workers into an embrace of middle-class values is practically an article of faith, even when it is portrayed as a missed opportunity, as in *Mary Barton,* when Mrs. Barton's death precipitates her husband's fall into Chartism, which is in effect a fall into lawlessness and, finally, murder.

The idea that tea improves the lot of workers both by providing them with an affordable pleasure and by making them more like, and thus more acceptable to, the middle class is persistent. But the unsustainability of this fantasy is revealed in an 1861 article in *Chambers's* titled "Tea." Tea is described as a drink all classes may enjoy, if not necessarily together; it is "a beverage destined to exert a world-wide influence on civilization, and in due time gladden every heart in [England], from that of its sovereign lady Queen Victoria down to that of humble Mrs Miff with her 'mortified bonnet.'"[56] In this formulation, the social scale is delimited by the queen of England on one end and a minor character (a pew-opener) from a Dickens novel, *Dombey and Son,* on the other. The fictional comfort of tea drinking among the poor has circled back around into the realm of journalistic reportage, yet the woman enjoying the comfort is a character in a book. Thus Queen Victoria escapes a concatenation that would inevitably connect her, no matter how distantly, with an actual member of the working class. Her imagined other is, in fact, imaginary. And the two hearts that stand in for "every heart" in England are women's hearts; the "taming" of men through tea is a process that must be mediated through women. "Indian Teas and Chinese Travellers" describes England, personified as John Bull, drinking tea "like a domesticated lion by the side of his elected Una . . . feeling himself proudly elevated by seeing her in her natural position, using her benignant influence for his best happiness."[57] Tea's power to forge links between the powerful and the powerless, a power that if real would potentially be profoundly destabilizing, is here contained by the familiar device of the matrimonial metaphor, in which influence is moral influence, influence without teeth.

Yet tea, as it privatizes the political, is linked with working women's education and literacy as well. The fearsome possibilities raised for eighteenth-century observers by women drinking tea together that Galt satirizes in his image of a coven of witches drinking brew shift in the nineteenth century so that the exchange of information among women is not corrosive (gossip) but positive (socially sanctioned forms of learning).[58] In *Jane Eyre* (1847), the semistarvation that Jane endures at Lowood Institution mirrors the intellectual and emotional privations she suffers there. As the narrator, Jane takes the reader methodically through a day's meals in order to impress upon us how the food seems perversely designed to weaken and demoralize the girls: burnt porridge for breakfast; rancid meat for dinner; half a slice of brown bread at five o'clock; oatcake and water before bed. Tea is brought in, but it is served only to the teachers. The one meal Jane shares with Miss Temple and Helen Burns takes on greater significance by contrast: not only is she comforted after being publicly humiliated by Mr. Brocklehurst, but she is fed seedcake and real tea: "And a tray was soon brought. How pretty, to my eyes, did the china cups and bright teapot look, placed on the little round table near the fire! How fragrant was the steam of the beverage, and the scent of the toast! . . . We feasted that evening as on nectar and ambrosia."[59]

The ostensible appeal of this scene (despite its unfortunate resemblance in tone to Gaskell's aforementioned Manchester tea party), which repeats itself when Jane once again finds shelter and comfort in the company of women at Moor House, is created in part by the multiple images of warmth (fire, tea, Miss Temple's embrace) but also through Jane's glowing admiration of the unexpected beauty of the tea things as a counterpart to the newly discovered beauty of her companion Helen Burns.

> The refreshing meal, the brilliant fire, the presence and kindness of her beloved instructress, or, perhaps, more than all these, something in her own unique mind, had roused her powers within her. They woke, they kindled: first, they glowed in the bright tint of her cheek . . . then they shone in the liquid lustre of her eyes, which had suddenly acquired a beauty more singular than that of Miss Temple's.[60]

Here are several elements of the tea mystique: to be given tea is to be nurtured, to drink it is to be soothed, comforted, or healed as the situation requires. Tea is also an intellectual stimulant, however, and its effect awakens Helen: "her soul sat on her lips, and language flowed, from what source I cannot tell. . . . They conversed of things I had never heard of; of nations and times past; of countries far away: of secrets of nature discovered or guessed at."[61] This too-brief scene of home comforts barely hints at what is to come. Helen's complexion is soon to take on the brilliance of late-stage tuberculosis, and she will die, leaving Jane to keep Helen alive in some sense by assimilating her intellectual powers while rejecting her passivity. Tea represents a set of unfulfilled possibilities—companionship, intellectual sympathy, material comfort—that Jane will pursue throughout the novel. When she finds Rochester, alone, blinded, and maimed, he is drinking water. In Gayatri Chakravorty Spivak's formulation, Jane's self-realization depends upon the death of Bertha Mason;[62] the enshrinement of tea as the embodiment of the domestic ideal even as it facilitates a certain circumscribed from of gendered education is conversely dependent on the persistent refusal to acknowledge an origin for tea outside the tea casket or caddy, where it is kept under lock and key, just as Bertha herself is locked away, not just from the rest of Thornfield, which is her rightful home, but from any history or context that might make meaning of her violence.[63]

The intertwined ideals of domesticity, service by and to the poor, and education that tea at different moments conjures up are crystallized in the character of Charley, the thirteen-year-old orphan in Charles Dickens's *Bleak House* who becomes Esther's maid after Jarndyce rescues her and her siblings. Charley is one of the many child characters that people Dickens's fiction whom he describes in *The Old Curiosity Shop* as having been "initiated into the ways of life, when they are scarcely more than infants," in consequence of which they are prematurely forced to "share our sorrows before they are capable of entering into our enjoyments."[64] When Charley's father dies, she is forced to work cleaning houses and doing laundry; she performs backbreaking adult labor, but because she is a child and the daughter of a debt collector, she is abused and underpaid by her employers. Charley's persecution by the Smallweeds, which echoes that of the childlike Trooper George, is crystallized in how she is given her tea.

> Judy [Smallweed] . . . begins to collect in a basin various tributary streams of tea, from the bottoms of cups and saucers and from the bottom of the teapot, for the little charwoman's evening meal. In like manner she gets together, in the iron bread-basket, as many outside fragments and worn-down heels of loaves as the rigid economy of the house has left in existence.[65]

Because the Smallweeds are obsessed with money to the exclusion of all else, their household is pervaded by such perversions of what should be home comforts: the furniture as well as the economy is rigid, the cushions are weapons, and the fire by which Grandfather Smallweed sits is not warm and cheerful but hot and oppressive, a foretaste of hellfire for the old usurer. Charley is forced to drink other people's leavings; her tea is that customarily destined for the slop bowl, also known as a slop basin, an adjunct to the tea service into which the cold dregs of the teacups and teapots were emptied before refilling. That the slop basin of the tea table shares its name with a container for excrement, also known as a slop jar, seems appropriate in this context; Charley is the remover of household dirt (in both senses of the word) in her capacity as charwoman and is thus marked physically by the Smallweeds' dirt and is fed their leavings. Like the word *dirt, slop* can mean mud or excrement in different contexts, and the *Oxford English Dictionary* uncharacteristically rolls these different meanings into one sense when it defines slop as "refuse liquid of any kind; rinsings of tea, coffee, or other beverages; the dirty water, etc., of a household."[66] (Much is contained in this "etc.," although the usage examples do little to clarify the point other than to cite the *Reminiscences* of Lady Bloomfield: "The slops had never been emptied, so the rooms were anything but odoriferous.") The feeding of children in Dickens's novels is always as much a matter of morals as nutrition, and to feed a worker who is also a child household refuse, as do the Smallweeds, is to fail to meet minimal standards of decency. The Smallweeds are thus meant to be understood as savage both because they mistreat orphans and because they cannot sit down to tea in a socially sanctioned manner.[67]

When Charley becomes Esther Summerson's maid, however, Esther both drinks tea with her and teaches her to read. Esther's illness and convalescence are bookended by scenes in which she describes drinking tea with Charley: her falling ill coincides with Charley's recovery, which is marked by Charley's ability to drink tea ("it was a great evening, when Charley and I at last took tea together").[68] After this brief happy scene, Esther herself is stricken with smallpox. Her emergence from the grip of the disease is marked by a similar event ("How well I remember the pleasant afternoon when I was raised in bed with pillows for the first time, to enjoy a great tea-drinking with Charley!").[69] These scenes suggest tea's ritual presence in the sickroom—the patient's ability to sit up and take tea often marks the shift from illness to convalescence[70]—but they also demonstrate the depth of sympathy between mistress and maid. As with Jane Eyre and Miss Temple, the tearoom is here a space of connection across boundaries of class, age, and authority. The ease with which these boundaries are transcended is remarkable in a novel in which such crossings are typically deadly; Esther contracts smallpox from Jo the crossing-sweeper and nearly dies, and her mother's class-climbing quasi-bigamous marriage to Sir Leicester Dedlock ends with her being hounded to her death by his lawyer Mr. Tulkinghorn, who is obsessed with forcing her secrets into the open. A measure of Lady Dedlock's com-promised identity is the degree to which she may be misread as her own maid, Hortense. The Chadbands' and Mrs. Pardiggle's ghastly attempts to save the souls of the poor are humiliating failures that succeed only in arousing fear in Jo and hostility in the brickmakers. Esther and Charley, however, bond, bound by their mutual debt of gratitude to Jarndyce, the financial benefactor of both. The seemingly uncomplicated nature of their relationship has its origin in the way that Charley enters Esther's life: Charley appears unannounced in Esther's room at Bleak House and explains that she is to be Esther's maid, saying, "If you please, miss, I'm a present to you, with Mr. Jarndyce's love. . . . I am a little present with his love, and it was all done for love of you."[71]

The gift of Charley, a transaction to which both object and recipient acquiesce without hesitation, is one of many such gifts that eventually convince Esther to make a gift of herself to Jarndyce although she loves another man. The novel figures Jarndyce as so magnanimous that he eventually (but without telling Esther) relinquishes claim to this gift and confers it upon Esther's beloved. Although Jarndyce leads Esther to be-lieve that he still intends to marry her, he secretly plots with the man he knows she loves to arrange their engagement. Revealing his plan at last, he claims Esther as his daughter and tells Allan Woodcourt to "take from me a willing gift, the best wife that ever man had. . . . Take with her the little home she brings you. . . . Allan, take my dear."[72]

Esther, then, can drink tea with Charley not because she is kind and Judy Smallweed is not, but because she understands herself to be simi-larly placed, a "willing gift" who deems her will to be of secondary im-portance to that of Jarndyce.[73] The woman-as-gift impinges upon but does not align with the woman-as-commodity; nevertheless, in the econ-omy of giving and exchange that marks the ritual of tea drinking, the gendered commodity and the commodification of gender converge.[74] The interiority of the "domestic" that John Tosh, following Davidoff and Hall, has shown to be overlaid with masculine presence, not to say au-thority,[75] is further structured by the presence of tea, the preparation of which reinforces and reifies Esther's and Charley's status as things to be given, women of "graceful affability and delicacy."[76] As mistress of Bleak House, the keeper of its keys, it is Esther's job to prepare tea for her guardian;[77] in this way she both presides and serves, making the home her world. Her labor, however, is mirrored in the pictures on the walls of "the whole process of preparing tea in China, as depicted by Chinese artists."[78] Similarly, Judy Smallweed's tea tray sounds like a "gong"; the specter of China arises unbidden, and tea refuses to remain fully domesticated. Seemingly sanctified and cleansed of its associations with the marketplace, tea nevertheless continues to signify in unexpected ways.

As in the eighteenth century, tea drinking is once again demonized in Sheridan LeFanu's 1868 ghost story "Green Tea." In the story, the excessive consumption of green tea, as opposed to black tea, works on the brain to rend the veil between the worlds of spirit and substance, so that a shy and studious clergyman is driven mad by the apparition of a monkey with glowing red eyes who follows him everywhere and torments him in church by sitting on his prayerbook to keep him from reading the service. The appearance of the monkey is linked not only with excess, but with writing and study as well—the clergyman, the Reverend Mr. Jennings, begins drinking green tea as he is working on a book treating "the religious metaphysics of the ancients."[79] He opines, "I believe, that every one who sets about writing in earnest does his work, as a friend of mine phrased it, *on* something—tea, or coffee, or tobacco."[80] The monkey eventually replaces the tea as Jennings's companion.

> Tea was my companion—at first the ordinary black tea, made in the usual way, not too strong: but I drank a good deal, and increased its strength as I went on. I never experienced an uncomfortable symptom from it. I began to take a little green tea. I found the effect pleasanter, it cleared and intensified the power of thought so, I had come to take it frequently, but not stronger than one might take it for pleasure.[81]

Here, black tea is deemed "ordinary"; green tea, conversely, is invested with both the power and the risks of a psychotropic drug that the narrator knows to be dangerous: "I began to take a little." The precise mechanism of action by means of which a drinker of green tea becomes a seer of devil-monkeys is difficult to determine from the narrative; LeFanu intersperses quotations from Emanuel Swedenborg's *Arcana Celestia*[82] with the narrator's own theories regarding the interconnectedness of the natural and spiritual worlds and his belief that "the essential man is a spirit [and] that the spirit is an organised substance, but as different in point of material from what we ordinarily understand by matter, as light or electricity is."[83] Finally, he explains that there exists a circulation arterial and venous in its mechanism, through the nerves. Of this system . . . the brain is the heart. The fluid, which is propagated hence through one class of nerves, returns in an altered state through another, and the nature of that fluid is spiritual, though not immaterial, any more than . . . light or electricity are so.

By various abuses, among which the habitual use of such agents as green tea is one, this fluid may be affected. . . . This fluid being that which we have in common with spirits, a congestion found upon the masses of brain or nerve, connected with the interior sense, forms a surface unduly exposed, on which disembodied spirits may operate: communication is thus more or less effectually established.[84]

The monkey, then, is not a hallucination, because tea does not cause hallucinations; rather, it is a genuine and particularly unpleasant spirit manifestation. Dr. Hessalius, the physician who fails to gain Jennings's confidence in time to save his life, claims to have encountered and cured "fifty-seven such cases,"[85] but he does not reveal the form the spirits took in these patients. The doctor here functions as exorcist, casting out demons from the possessed. But it is worth noting that in the *Arcana Celestia,* Swedenborg's spirits frequently take pleasant or at least nonthreatening forms, while the more malignant, beastly spirits are associated with vice.[86] So in the story's terms, the monkey is both a physiological result of drinking tea and a sort of punishment for having done so.

While the medical discourse in "Green Tea" may be unique to the subject, treatises warning the middle class of the dangers of green tea dated back at least to the eighteenth century. Yet by 1868 tea was no longer thought to be injurious to the health, and the locus of anxiety over contact with India and China had shifted. Asia was still the focus of nightmares and fantasies of adventure, death, and danger, but tea, having been grown or bought and shipped by the English, was by this time more or less understood to be English. LeFanu himself calls tea the English "national beverage"[87] in "Carmilla."

Why then is LeFanu invoking a set of beliefs about tea with which his readers might well have been unfamiliar? Hessalius learns that Jennings's close friend, Lady Mary, has argued with him over his tea-drinking habit, which she apparently persuaded him at last to give up. This is an odd occurrence regarding a beverage whose literary role is generally to prompt good fellowship rather than fracture longstanding friendships. One possible explanation may be found by reading "Green Tea" through the lens of Thomas De Quincey's *Confessions of an English Opium-Eater,* which LeFanu read as a young man.[88] In "Green Tea," the frame narrative dates the case notes from "sixty-four years ago," or in the first decade of the nineteenth century. So historically, the time is right for this kind of speculation on tea. It also places the events in "Green Tea" close to the 1813 date of "the pains of opium" section of the *Confessions.* In "Introduction to the Pains of Opium," De Quincey describes how for several years prior to 1813 he had been living in the Lake District, taking opium and studying "German metaphysics" (83)[89] with no apparent ill effects, until, to treat an illness, he began eating opium daily, and his "pains" commenced. Around this time, an odd incident occurred; seemingly out of nowhere, a "Malay" knocked at his door and the young servant who answered the knock "gave me to understand that there was a sort of demon below" with "sallow and bilious skin" and "small, fierce, restless eyes."[90] Unable to communicate, De Quincey gives the man what he thinks are several doses' worth of opium, which the Malay eats all at once as he leaves. De Quincey is both consumed by curiosity (What was the mysterious stranger doing here? What did he want?) and racked by guilt that he may have inadvertently killed his visitor with an overdose of opium. He writes that the Malay "fastened afterwards upon my dreams and brought other Malays with him worse than himself that ran *amok* at me and led me into a world of trouble";[91] by 1818, despite periods of respite, the Malay still haunts his dreams nightly and has been "a fearful enemy for months," bringing with him all the horrors De Quincey associates with "Southern Asia . . . the seat of awful images and associations."[92] The Malay, then, is both a living embodiment of opium itself and its (fantasy) place of origin (south Asia as Hell). He is also the avatar of the pains of opium, a malicious demon who stalks De Quincey's dreams, the personification of the monkey on his back.[93] In all of the other stories in which LeFanu explores the theme of a man with a guilty conscience being driven mad by a figure that stalks him, the figure is a small, ugly foreign man ("The Watcher" and "The Fortunes of Sir Robert Ardagh" are two examples); furthermore, a variation of the term "having a monkey on your back" is "having a chinaman on your back."[94] All in all, "Green Tea" would perhaps make more sense, both to a reader in 1872 and to us, if we replaced the words *green tea* with *opium.*

So as black tea begins to compete with opium as the cash crop cultivated by the British in India,[95] and as Indian commodities become increasingly "domesticated," both in the sense that their place of origin is dislodged from their social meaning and in the sense that they are more British, or at least more under British ownership and control, green tea loses its primacy as the English national beverage and again becomes something vaguely foreign and malevolent. Following this move in his fiction, LeFanu appropriates the discourse of opium addiction, grafts it onto eighteenth-century arguments about the pernicious influence of tea on the nerves, and moves the entire construct out of the realm of the material—a term used with contempt in "Green Tea"—and into that of Swedenborgian metaphysics. But "Green Tea" is the counterexample. The "national beverage" remains, inside the homes inside the novels, locked in its casket, its status as an idea finally as unaltered as its change of origin is unmarked.

CHAPTER FIVE

Imperial Imports at the Fin de Siècle

By the end of the nineteenth century, the domestic novel was on the wane as a genre, and literary depictions of Indian material culture looked substantially different. A case in point: Arthur Conan Doyle's novella *The Sign of Four* (1890) is explicitly an imperial detective story, and like its literary predecessor *The Moonstone* is a tale of ill-gotten Indian treasure.[1] The home of Thaddeus Sholto, the son of the army officer who has brought a chest full of stolen jewels back to England, is in a suburb of London, but it is utterly unlike the "Bran-new" houses of upper-middle-class social strivers, full of hideous new English furnishings, that Dickens mocks in *Our Mutual Friend* (1864), or even the pathetically banal suburban home of the clerk Charles Pooter satirized by George and Weedon Grossmith in *Diary of a Nobody,* which was first serialized in *Punch* in 1888–89.[2] In Thaddeus's nightmarishly Eastern home, "valuable curiosities" from India have replaced proper English decor just as Eastern habits of dress and behavior have pushed aside proper English deportment. No longer novelties, status symbols, or conversation pieces, and not in the least domesticated, Sholto's possessions and clothing, as well as his "Eastern" habits, are marks of corruption and contagion.

At least since the publication of Judith Walkowitz's *City of Dreadful Delight,* contemporary critics have recognized the trend toward depictions of urban menace in fin de siècle novels and stories. The threat may come from the urban underclass, as in Walter Besant's *All Sorts and Conditions of Men,* or it may emerge from a sense of Continental corruption, as in Bram Stoker's *Dracula.*[3] What is striking is that in contradistinction to the midcentury domestic novel, imperial foreignness is now frequently embodied by human characters rather than mediated through commodities. Yet as the example of Thaddeus Sholto illustrates, the bodies that figure the danger of the un-English need not necessarily be foreign; they may, paradoxically, be English by birth. As Yumna Siddiqi has demonstrated in her analysis of the Sherlock Holmes stories, "returned colonials are portrayed as menacing, and their presence in England precipitates a crisis, either a crime or a mysterious tragedy."[4] The oddity of these characters is frequently reinforced by the outlandish people, animals, and/or things that have accompanied them back to England. In *The Sign of Four,* the initial mystery that Holmes is called upon to solve, one that becomes infinitely more convoluted as the case progresses, is at once straightforward and redolent of Oriental secrets: A young English woman named Mary Morstan is contacted by her father upon his return from a lengthy tour of duty as an officer in charge of the convict-guard on the Andaman Islands. She travels to London to meet him, but he has disappeared, leaving behind a suitcase containing clothes, books, and "a considerable number of curiosities from the Andaman Islands."[5] Four years after his disappearance, she receives a large and valuable pearl in the mail; each year on the same date she receives another. She contacts Holmes when her mysterious benefactor asks to meet her; the ensuing adventure leads Holmes, Watson, and Mary Morstan to the home of Thaddeus Sholto, the son of Morstan's fellow officer and closest friend. Thaddeus has moved out of his father's opulent home, now occupied by his brother Bartholomew, and into this suburban wasteland. As Holmes dryly observes, "our quest does not appear to take us to very fashionable regions." Watson elaborates:

> We had indeed reached a questionable and forbidding neighbourhood. Long lines of dull brick houses were only relieved by the coarse glare and tawdry brilliancy of public-houses at the corner. Then came rows of two-storied villas, each with a fronting of miniature garden, and then again interminable lines of new, staring brick buildings—the monster tentacles which the giant city was throwing out into the country. At last the cab drew up at the third house in a new terrace. None of the other houses were inhabited, and that at which we stopped was as dark as its neighbours, save for a single glimmer in the kitchen-window. On our knocking, however, the door was instantly thrown open by a Hindoo servant, clad in a yellow turban, white loose-fitting clothes, and a yellow sash.

> There was something strangely incongruous in this Oriental figure
> framed in the commonplace doorway of a third-rate suburban dwelling-
> house.[6]

Here, newness is conflated with monstrosity and danger, and as the
figure of the Indian servant framed in the doorway suggests, Indian trea-
sure/plunder comes with or is followed by human counterparts, as in *The
Moonstone*. The inclusion of Indian and Andamanese people, in addition
to things, suggests at once that England's imperial holdings can no longer
be looked at solely as blank spaces for the extraction of wealth and that
this more complex view of imperial undertakings is deeply troubling. At
the same time, however, the threat of imperial contagion has to some degree been kept away from the mainstream of metropolitan life in both
the topographic and social senses. It has been isolated, not in an inner-
city slum, but at the outer limits of the city dwellers' knowledge of geography or ideas of respectability. Both Jonathan Small and Major Sholto
have been turned into thieves and murderers by their encounter with
South Asia, but they pose a danger only to the small circle of family
members and co-conspirators in which they remain embedded to the exclusion of the outside world.

As in Collins's text, history intrudes explicitly in the plot: during the
Indian Rebellion of 1857, three Sikhs conspire with a white man,
Jonathan Small, to murder a rajah's emissary and steal a chest of jewels.
The four are convicted of the emissary's murder, although the authorities
do not learn of the chest's existence, and are sent to prison on the Andaman Islands. They reveal their secret to two officers, Morstan and
Sholto, in the hope of buying their freedom, but Sholto deceives them
all, steals the treasure, and returns to England, where he ensconces himself in a house called Pondicherry Lodge with bodyguards and an Indian
butler, Lal Chowdar. When Morstan returns to England and demands
his share of the treasure, Sholto kills him (whether accidentally or not remains an open question) and disposes of Morstan's body with the help of
Lal Chowdar. Small eventually escapes from prison with the help of an
Andaman Islander named Tonga whose life he has saved, and they make
their way to England to exact revenge on Sholto. We later learn, however,
that Lal Chowdar is not as loyal as he first appears: he has given Jonathan
Small regular intelligence on the household. Small is secretly summoned
to the house twice through these means: once when Sholto is on his

deathbed, and again as soon as the treasure is found by his son Bartholomew,[7] the occurrence that prompts Thaddeus Sholto to contact Mary Morstan. On his second visit, Small is able to steal the jewel chest, but Tonga disobeys his orders and kills Bartholomew hours before Thaddeus arrives with Holmes, Watson, and Mary. The presence of imperial subjects in England thus signals to the English the arrival of double-crossing, revenge, and death. The standard British mutiny narrative of English trust and Indian treachery is reversed in that an English officer betrays three Indians and steals their treasure, but the moral of the story seems only to be that everyone connected with India will eventually suffer for it. The English characters, Small, Morstan, and Sholto, must return to England to pay privately for their crimes, whereas their Indian co-conspirators are fixed in place in a colonial island prison as a result of British justice, neither here nor there.

To return to the homes of Thaddeus and Bartholomew Sholto: the interior of Thaddeus's home is in striking contrast to the "howling desert of South London" (100) in which it is situated. As Watson describes it:

> We were all astonished by the appearance of the apartment into which he invited us. In that sorry house it looked as out of place as a diamond of the first water in a setting of brass. The richest and glossiest of curtains and tapestries draped the walls, looped back here and there to expose some richly mounted painting or Oriental vase. The carpet was of amber and black, so soft and so thick that the foot sank pleasantly into it, as into a bed of moss. Two great tiger-skins thrown athwart it increased the suggestion of Eastern luxury, as did a huge hookah which stood upon a mat in the corner. A lamp in the fashion of a silver dove was hung from an almost invisible golden wire in the centre of the room. As it burned it filled the air with a subtle and aromatic odour.[8]

Here diamonds are invoked only through simile, and the tapestries (textiles) are merely gestured at. The crucial point being made is that every surface, every aspect of the room is implicated in its Indianization: an Indian lamp hangs from the ceiling; Oriental paintings, curtains, and tapestries cover the walls; the Eastern carpets underfoot are accentuated with tiger skins. The very air is perfumed with Oriental incense and tobacco smoke from the hookah. Yet Thaddeus, despite his aestheticized affect, has exiled himself from the family home, Pondicherry Lodge, because of his adherence to the presumably English values of chivalry and fair play. (Thaddeus desires to share the Indian treasure with Mary Morstan, whom he feels to be a rightful claimant.) Christopher Keep and Don Randall have argued that in this scene, the "disruptive force of the Indian Mutiny is signified . . . by its capacity to transform the space of the metropole, of London itself, into a version of its unmapped and un-knowable place of origin, the colonial periphery."[9] The center/periphery model comes undone in what Keep and Randall describe as the collapse of distinctions in Sholto's apartment, a "confusing world of free-floating signs of race and nationality, in which the 'suburban' becomes the 'exotic' and vice versa."[10] I would push their point further, however, to argue that the "mutiny" as disruptive force only serves to stand in for a much longer narrative; it is not simply the events of 1857 but the entire sweep of the history of British India from the battle of Plassey (1757) forward that is evoked in such scenes, and Thaddeus himself represents the survival of an earlier type of imperialist who embraced Indian dress and customs, as I discuss in chapter 1. His incorrect relationship to empire, which in the story's structure cannot be uncoupled from his repellent and un-English physical appearance, provides sufficient narrative justification for his identical twin's murder by a similarly small and repellent character, the Andamanese Islander Tonga.

Upon entering Pondicherry Lodge, Holmes and Watson discover Bartholomew Sholto's dead body as well as evidence including small footprints, a stone hammer, and a poisoned dart found in the murdered man's head. Holmes immediately deduces that one of the suspects is from the Andaman Islands, and he reads to Watson from a gazetteer that he considers "the very latest authority."

> [Andamanese] are naturally hideous, having large, misshapen heads, small fierce eyes, and distorted features. . . . So intractable and fierce are they, that all the efforts of the British officials have failed to win them over in any degree. They have always been a terror to shipwrecked crews, braining the survivors with their stone-headed clubs or shooting them with their poisoned arrows. These massacres are invariably concluded by a cannibal feast.[11]

As John McBratney has noted in his reading of the *The Sign of Four,* while this description is clearly Doyle's invention and in many aspects flatly contradicts accounts by contemporary anthropologists, the "under-lying concepts" in Doyle's imaginary gazetteer "match those that undergird the physical anthropology of [Indian Census Commissioner Herbert H.] Risley and others. Most of the central concepts associated with racial type—essence, fixity, distinctiveness, [and] reversion . . . are reflected here."[12] McBratney further links the concept of the racial type to that of the criminal type to argue that both discourses converge in the character of Tonga, the Andamanese murderer, and that Holmes and Tonga represent "opposite end[s] of the human scale"[13] who nevertheless share uncanny similarities. What divides them, ultimately, is that Holmes is presented as a unique and special example of English manhood whereas Tonga is exactly like others of his kind. Holmes's famous "science of deduction,"[14] which he demonstrates in *Sign of Four* by performing an analysis of a pocket-watch, allows him to intuit details unique to the individual; in this case, he observes that the watch's owner was "a man of untidy habits . . . [who] was left with good prospects, but he threw away his chances, lived for some time in poverty with occasional short intervals of prosperity, and finally, taking to drink . . . died."[15] Naturally, Holmes is correct on all points. To read the possessions of an Englishman is to learn about *him;* to read the possessions of an Andamanese is to identify him as a member of a "race" (in the nineteenth-century sense of the term), a designation that provides all of the information necessary to understand and, presumably, to bring him to justice (although Holmes and Watson shoot Tonga rather than apprehending him). Similarly, when Watson meets Mary Morstan, the woman he is to marry, he describes her unique qualities: "Her expression was sweet and amiable, and her large blue eyes were singularly spiritual and sympathetic. In an experience of women which extends over many nations and three separate continents, I have never looked upon a face which gave a clearer promise of a refined and sensitive nature."[16] Conversely, he calls Tonga's face "enough to give a man a sleepless night. Never have I seen features so deeply marked with all bestiality and cruelty."[17] Both faces, then, are singular in Watson's experience, as marked by the word *never,* yet Tonga's is terrifying in its conformity to type. When the practice of "reading" migrates from things to faces, it moves in some sense from the material to the metaphysical, yet the results are the same. Tonga's face tells essentially the same story as his weapons.

The phobic response to Indian furnishings similar to those that functioned as avatars of good taste in Gaskell's *Wives and Daughters* (which I discuss in chapter 2) as well as to people intimately connected with South

Asia raises the question, Why the radical change in signification? It would be easy to claim that what were seen more widely by late-century writers as the evils attendant on the imperial enterprise came to inhere in the spoils of the East, but this is far too simple a formulation. The will to impose meaning on objects takes many forms, and in *The Sign of Four,* Doyle uses "eastern" objects within the suburban household to signal among other things Thaddeus Sholto's refusal of convention and his embrace of aestheticism. Indian material culture takes on new connotations once it is associated with aestheticism and decadence, even as a minor plot device: Indian things are reestablished as something exotic and outré but also mystical, a resonance that was revived in the 1960s and continues to reverberate into the present day.[18] Yet despite this mystification, things carry with them a history that cannot be so easily effaced. Burdened with his father's imperial inheritance, Thaddeus attempts to transform it into metropolitan "style" but fails, just as Franklin Blake in *The Moonstone* fails to transform a sacred diamond into a piece of domestic jewelry and Godfrey Ablewhite fails to turn it into a commodity. Taste is revealed once again to be far more than a private matter, but a highly charged means of mediating if not subsuming political, economic, and cultural forces.

In a related vein, Oscar Wilde studs the opening scene of *The Picture of Dorian Gray* with non-Western artifacts that signify the presence of a fin de siècle aesthetic sensibility: the novel opens on Lord Henry Wotton in the painter Basil Hallward's studio, reclining on a "divan of Persian saddlebags,"[19] smoking "opium-tainted"[20] cigarettes, and observing how the shadows of birds in flight, visible through translucent "tussore-silk" (Indian) curtains, produce "a kind of momentary Japanese effect."[21] All of the senses are invoked here except that of touch, because Dorian has not arrived, and it is Dorian who is to be touched by Henry, to be tainted with new ideas and seduced into the knowledge that will transform his life utterly. Dorian is infected not only by the ideas conveyed through Lord Henry's words but by promises of worldly knowledge to come that are evoked by the material objects that surround him in the studio. Eventually, he will take to an extreme the experiences at which Basil's things gesture obliquely: he will smoke opium in the foulest of East End opium dens, amass priceless collections of art and textiles, and, presumably, participate in the orgies that in contemporaneous pornographic novels inevitably take place in similarly Orientalized settings.[22] In an artfully staged moment in the second chapter, Henry approaches Dorian, whose face is buried in a lilac bush, places his hand on Dorian's shoulder, and murmurs, "Nothing can cure the soul but the senses, just as nothing can cure the senses but the soul."[23] The artist's studio as temple of the senses, touched with suggestions of Orientalist decadence, is figured as a dangerous space; even the "small Japanese table"[24] on which Basil Hallward serves tea, gesturing as it does toward a world of rarefied tastes and hedonistic pleasures, carries an entirely different resonance than did the British-made "japanned" tea tray that lends an air of cozy domesticity to the working-class tea party in Elizabeth Gaskell's 1848 novel *Mary Barton* that I discuss in chapter 4. Japan-ware, as japanned goods were also known, was manufactured commercially, most famously in Birmingham, but versions of japan-ware were also painted at home by English women and could thus be considered a part of the midcentury craze for homemade crafts that, as Talia Schaffer explains, "declined after 1870, when the Arts and Crafts movement introduced a new and very different understanding of craft, privileging marks of handmade individual skilled artistry instead of the cheerfully amateurish knickknacks produced by domestic handicraft makers following mass-produced instructions."[25] Before the "opening" of Japan by the United States in 1854 and the signing of the Tianjin treaty by Lord Elgin in 1858, Japan existed only as a misty entity in the British imagination, fed mainly, as Toshio Yokoyama has demonstrated, by rehashed sixteenth-century travelers' accounts.[26] Yet by the 1870s, new books as well as articles in such magazines as *Cornhill* and *Blackwood's* were available to the reading public,[27] many of which insisted upon the ethereal strangeness and beauty of Japan and the Japanese people. Japan thus begins to replace a now too-familiar India as the source of exoticized "status" commodities. Such Japanese exports as teapots, tea, and silk textiles were beginning to be seen in middle-class English homes by the 1870s, and British writers routinely praised what Sir Cyprian Bridge, a commander in the Royal Navy who published several essays on Japan in the popular press, called in 1878 "That style of art which was founded on the observation of Nature, which followed Nature in all of the richness of her luxuriant variety."[28] Adherents of the Aesthetic movement, however, embraced rarer examples of Japanese painting and decorative arts than those available to the middle class, while Wilde himself explicitly rejected the notion that Japanese art was founded on nature.

In Wilde's essay "The Decay of Lying," his narrator Vivian objects to British realist fiction as inevitably "vulgarizing"[29] to the degree that it attempts to draw directly from real life. "We have mistaken the common livery of the age for the vesture of the Muses,"[30] he claims, arguing that art should transform life into "purely imaginative and pleasurable work dealing with what is unreal and non-existent."[31] Imitation of ordinary life can only produce ordinary art, and it is not the artist's duty to "draw public attention to the state of our convict prisons, and the management of our private lunatic asylums";[32] that is the work of politicians, journalists, and pamphleteers. To illustrate his point, Vivian turns to the decorative arts.

> What is true about drama and the novel is no less true about those arts that we call decorative arts. The whole history of these arts in Europe is the record of the struggle between Orientalism, with its frank rejection of imitation, its love of artistic convention, its dislike to the actual representation of any object in Nature, and our own imitative spirit. Wherever the former has been paramount, as in Byzantium, Sicily, and Spain, by actual contact, or in the rest of Europe by the influence of the Crusades, we have had beautiful and imaginative work in which the visible things of life are transmuted into artistic conventions, and the things that Life has not are invented and fashioned for her delight. But wherever we have returned to Life and Nature, our work has always become vulgar, common, and uninteresting.[33]

He goes on to explain how "lying" for its own sake is for this reason necessary to art, and that the best styles of any age or place are not imitative but ideal: "No great artist ever sees things as they really are. If he did, he would cease to be an artist."[34] To this end, Vivian asserts that the Japan represented in Japanese art bears no resemblance whatever to an actual landscape or actual people, and that Japan as the British imagine it "is a pure invention."[35]

It is perhaps unsurprising that the next example to which Vivian turns is that of ancient Greece: "Do you think that Greek art ever tells us what the Greek people were like?"[36] Ancient Greece and the non-West are frequently paired in Wilde's writing; in *Dorian Gray*, for example, as Dorian sits for his fateful portrait in Basil Hallward's Orientalized studio, Lord Henry expounds on the "Hellenic ideal" of living life "fully and completely," of giving "form to every feeling, expression to every thought, reality to every dream."[37] This of course is the speech that first works a change in Dorian's consciousness, and critics have decisively linked Wilde's use of ancient Greece in the novel (and elsewhere) to his rhetoric of homoeroticism.[38] Yet the example of Japanese and Oriental (in this context Near Eastern) art suggests that Japanese aesthetics as adumbrated in "Decay" are not unrelated to *Dorian Gray*'s sexual politics. In arguing that life and even nature imitate art, Wilde is gesturing toward the possibility of a life that breaks decisively with life as represented in mid-Victorian novels, that refuses a slavish imitation of that most evergreen of realist-novel conventions, the marriage plot. Life, in other words, may be drawn from an artistic tradition or style in which people do not look (or, by extension, act) like people as they are assumed to be by the middle-class moralizers who write realist novels. Thus the Hellenic ideal is given theoretical underpinning by an artistic tradition the value of which inheres for Wilde in its resistance to appropriation by a heteronormative middle class in search of its own idealized reflection. Furthermore, Dorian himself represents an ideal form: a Tithonus in reverse who possesses perpetual youth but not immortality, Dorian is a work of art who possesses "beauty such as old Greek marbles kept for us."[39] In his looks and in his life, Dorian diverges from ordinary men in precisely the way that Wilde shows Japanese art to be incommensurate with "nature."

Orientalism similar to that in *Dorian Gray* is everywhere apparent in the late-Victorian *Teleny,* the 1893 pornographic novel in which Wilde is widely believed to have had a hand either as one of several writers, as editor, or both.[40] Again, though, the Middle East and the Far East feature far more prominently than India, and the famous orgy scene in the painter Briancourt's studio brings into sharp focus the semiotics of Basil Hallward's studio in *Dorian Gray:* standing on a balcony "made out of old Arabic *moucharaby,*"[41] the narrator Des Grieux observes, by the light of Japanese and Moorish lamps, a room below in which young men recline "on faded old damask couches, on huge pillows made out of priests' stoles, worked by devout fingers in silver and in gold, on soft Persian and Syrian divans, on lion and panther rugs . . . in attitudes of the most consummate lewdness . . . such as are only seen in the brothels of men in lecherous Spain, or in those of the wanton East."[42] The studio itself is "a museum of lewd art worthy of Sodom or of Babylon."[43] As Robert Gray and Christopher Keep observe, "for queer writers [in fin de siècle England] the East is less a place on the map than it is a kind of virtual space in which they can imagine a sexuality beyond that prescribed within the normative confines of the domestic realist novel."[44] While this is undoubtedly true, the profusion of Eastern objects as well as the presence of actual Arabs at Briancourt's orgy suggests that more may be at stake; in addition, the repeated invocation of London as either Sodom or Babylon in gay guidebooks and pornography of the period suggests that these geographic coordinates possessed significance beyond their ostensible biblical referents. The "virtual space" of the East must always be instantiated and propped up through the realm of the material, even if the spoils of empire are depicted as priceless treasures or ancient plunder rather than vulgar commodities from everyday shops. Furthermore, as Robert Aldrich and most recently Anjali Arondekar have demonstrated, the fantasy of the East as a homoerotic paradise was based in part on accounts of what Europeans were actually doing in the colonies, particularly North Africa and India.[45]

Again, though, Indian things have been displaced to a large degree by those of Japan, the Middle East, and North Africa in the late-century discourse of decadence, and with the exception of tea, they have largely disappeared in more mainstream fiction. The disappearance of Indian material objects from novels simply means that their meanings have changed; far from having vanished, they continue to circulate in Western culture in ways that both resonate with and break from their past lives as colonial commodities. Today Tipu Sultan's throne, along with his infamous mechanical tiger and other personal effects, is on display at the Victoria and Albert Museum in London. The Koh-i-noor diamond has been recut and mounted in the Queen Mother's crown, which may be seen with the other crown jewels in the Tower of London. Although most Kashmir shawls have long since been consigned to dust, a surprising number live on in the collections of several of the world's major art museums and are beginning to be reclassified as examples of Islamic art, which they certainly are; so-called pashmina shawls of varying fabrics and quality are sold everywhere in the United States from exclusive boutiques to department stores to street fairs. Despite coffee's challenge to its hegemony, tea remains both solidly popular worldwide and subject to widely varying claims about its effects on the body, although British colonial rule has meant that tea production has been globalized and now takes place in other former colonies including Sri Lanka and Kenya.

Under Mohandas Gandhi, homespun Indian cloth (*khadi*) became the centerpiece of the anticolonial swadeshi (self-sufficiency) movement, which was symbolized by the spinning wheel, or *charkha;* so potent was the charkha as an avatar of India's need to reclaim what it had lost that it appeared on the first flag of the Indian National Congress as early as 1921. For politicians, activists, and ordinary people alike, to wear khadi was to make a powerful political statement against both British rule and the imported textiles that the colonial government had imposed on the nation. Nationalist movements were brutally suppressed by the British government and their members frequently imprisoned at Fort Blair in the Andaman Islands, which became known as the "Indian Bastille" for its preponderance of political prisoners. Although India gained independence in 1947, the violence and chaos that accompanied Partition, occurring as they did in the aftermath of World War II, were barely registered by much of the Western world despite the fact that Partition created twelve million refugees, and between five hundred thousand and one million people are estimated to have died. Yet twenty years later, inexpensive South Asian textiles and clothing, along with yoga, incense, and sitar music, would become fashionable in England and the United States with various youth countercultural movements of the 1960s and 1970s, among whom travel to India became a status symbol. British musicians made highly publicized trips to South Asia in search of gurus and spiritual enlightenment,[46] and the old colonial mystifications were reenacted on a somewhat different stage at precisely the moment that the 1962 Commonwealth Immigrants Act and the 1965 Immigration and Nationality Act allowed unprecedented numbers of South Asians into Great Britain and the United States respectively.

Today, *khadi* production in India is protected and promoted by the Khadi and Village Industries Commission established by Parliament in 1957, and textile workers are eagerly sought out by NGOs and aid organizations to be organized into collectives and/or offered microcredit. The endurance of these forms of South Asian material culture, however remarkable, must nevertheless be read in terms of the ruptures engendered by imperialism and Western capitalism in the nineteenth century, the histories of which inhere and survive in the representations of the Indian things that litter nineteenth-century cultural production.

Notes

1. Charles Dickens, *Our Mutual Friend* (New York: Penguin Classics, 1997), 17.

2. Dickens, *Our Mutual Friend,* 792. The word *job* as a verb is multiply suggestive here; it can mean "to get (a person) into a position corruptly or unscrupulously," to "deal out (an asset or commodity) for profit," or to "To pierce or poke (a person or thing) with a brief, forceful action, usually with the end or point of something; to stab, peck, prod, or jab" (*OED*). That is to say that Veneering has gone too vigorously at the opportunities for corruption (jobberies) that his seat in Parliament has opened for him. Dickens uses the term more literally in the latter sense in *Martin Chuzzlewit* when he writes that the monstrous Hannibal Chollop was "greatly beloved for the gallant manner in which he had 'jobbed out' the eye of one gentleman, as he was in the act of knocking at his own street-door" (492).

3. Dickens, *Our Mutual Friend,* 84.

4. Dickens, *Our Mutual Friend,* 302.

5. In nineteenth-century fiction, *Hindoo* could refer either to the Hindu religion or to Indian identity; Indians and Hindus were thus frequently collapsed into one category.

6. Annette B. Weiner, "Cultural Difference and the Density of Objects," *American Ethnologist* 21 (1993): 394.

7. There are, of course, exceptions to this rule, although the majority of Indian characters in mid-Victorian novels are male servants who function as stock figures. For a history of Indian people in Great Britain in the nineteenth century, see Rozina Visram, *Asians in Britain: 400 Years of History* (London: Pluto, 2002). The problematic term *domestic fiction* is generally used over and against sensation fiction; in this context I would oppose it as well to detective fiction and adventure novels, both of which are more likely than domestic fiction to feature non-English people.

8. Ranajit Guha, *History at the Limit of World-History* (New York: Columbia University Press, 2002), 9–10. Guha quotes Hegel: "It is obvious to anyone with even a rudimentary knowledge of the treasures of Indian literature that this country, so rich in spiritual achievements of a truly profound quality, *has no history*" (9; emphasis in original).

9. For more on this topic in a domestic context, see Ruth Richardson, *Death, Dissection, and the Destitute* (Chicago: University of Chicago Press, 2001), especially chapter 1, "The Corpse and Popular Culture."

10. Fredric Jameson, *The Modernist Papers* (London: Verso, 2007), 157.

11. Raymond Williams, *The Country and the City* (New York: Oxford University Press, 1975), 165.

12. Jameson, *The Modernist Papers*, 156.

13. Bill Brown, *The Material Unconscious: American Amusement, Stephen Crane, and the Economies of Play* (Cambridge: Harvard University Press, 1996), 4.

14. I am thinking of, for example, Antoinette Burton, *Burdens of History: British Feminists, Indian Women, and Imperial Culture, 1865–1915* (Chapel Hill: University of North Carolina Press, 1994); *Western Women and Imperialism: Complicity and Resistance,* ed. Nupur Chaudhuri and Margaret Stroebel (Bloomington: Indiana University Press, 1992); Deirdre David, *Rule Britannia: Women, Empire, and Victorian Writing* (Ithaca: Cornell University Press, 1995); Inderpal Grewal, *Home and Harem: Nation, Gender, Empire, and the Cultures of Travel* (Durham: Duke University Press, 1996), which deals with both England and India; Lata Mani, *Contentious Traditions: The Debate on Sati in Colonial India* (Berkeley: University of California Press, 1998); Jenny Sharpe, *Allegories of Empire: The Figure of Woman in the Colonial Text* (Minneapolis: University of Minnesota Press, 1993); Rajeswari Sunder Rajan, *Real and Imagined Women: Gender, Culture, and Postcolonialism* (London: Routledge, 1993); and Gauri Viswanathan, *Masks of Conquest: Literary Study and British Rule in India* (Delhi: Oxford University Press, 1998).

15. Gayatri Chakravorty Spivak's "Three Women's Texts and a Critique of Imperialism" was one of the earliest and certainly the most influential of these interventions; a recent example of such work by historians is Catherine Hall and Sonya O. Rose's edited collection *At Home with the Empire: Metropolitan Culture and the Imperial World* (Cambridge: Cambridge University Press, 2006). Others include Daniel Bivona, *Desire and Contradiction: Imperial Visions and Domestic Debates in Victorian Literature* (Manchester: Manchester University Press, 1990), Susan Meyer, *Imperialism at Home: Race and Victorian Women's Fiction* (Ithaca: Cornell University Press, 1996), Barry Milligan, *Pleasures and Pains: Opium and the Orient in Nineteenth-Century British Culture* (Charlottesville: University of Virginia Press, 1995), and Timothy Carens, *Outlandish English Subjects in the Victorian Domestic Novel* (Houndsmills, Basingstoke: Palgrave Macmillan, 2005).

16. Elaine Freedgood, *The Ideas in Things: Fugitive Meaning in the Victorian Novel* (Chicago: University of Chicago Press, 2006), 1 (emphasis in original).

17. Freedgood, *The Ideas in Things*, 1, 2.

18. Freedgood, *The Ideas in Things,* 2.

19. Bill Brown, *A Sense of Things: The Object Matter of American Literature* (Chicago: University of Chicago Press, 2003), 4.

20. Patrick Brantlinger, *Rule of Darkness: British Literature and Imperialism, 1830–1914* (Ithaca: Cornell University Press, 1988), 34.

21. Brantlinger, *Rule of Darkness,* 38.

22. Conversely, as John Kucich observes, novels helped to shape public opinion on and beliefs about imperialism; see *Imperial Masochism: British Fiction, Fantasy, and Social Class* (Princeton: Princeton University Press, 2006), 15.

23. Leonore Davidoff and Catherine Hall's *Family Fortunes: Men and Women of the English Middle Class, 1780–1850* (Chicago: University of Chicago Press, 1987) remains an authoritative narrative of this phenomenon. See especially part 2, chapter 6, and part 3, chapter 8.

24. Brown, *A Sense of Things,* 13.

25. Brown, *A Sense of Things,* 5.

26. Arjun Appadurai, Introduction, *The Social Life of Things: Commodities in Cultural Perspective,* ed. Arjun Appadurai (Cambridge: Cambridge University Press, 1986), 5.

27. Karl Marx, *Capital: A Critique of Political Economy,* vol. 1, trans. Ben Fowkes (New York: Penguin, 1990), 163–77. Marx states that "the definite social relation between men themselves . . . assumes here, for them, the fantastic form of a relation between things. . . . I call this the fetishism which attaches itself to the products of labour as soon as they are produced as commodities" (165).

28. Byron Farwell, *Queen Victoria's Little Wars* (New York: Norton, 1972).

29. Aamir Mufti and Ella Shohat, Introduction, *Dangerous Liaisons: Gender, Nation, and Postcolonial Perspectives,* ed. Anne McClintock, Aamir Mufti, and Ella Shohat (Minneapolis: University of Minnesota Press, 1997), 1.

30. See, for example, Davidoff and Hall, *Family Fortunes,* especially chapter 8. See also Maura Ives, "Housework, Mill Work, Women's Work: The Functions of Cloth in Charlotte Brontë's *Shirley,*" in *Keeping the Victorian House: A Collection of Essays,* ed. Vanessa D. Dickerson (New York: Garland, 1995).

31. Gayatri Spivak, *A Critique of Postcolonial Reason: Toward a History of the Vanishing Present* (Cambridge: Harvard University Press, 1999), 199.

32. Teresa Hubel, *Whose India? The Independence Struggle in British and Indian Fiction and History* (Durham: Duke University Press, 1996), 1.

CHAPTER I

1. Later-nineteenth-century Kashmir shawls were often made up either of a central piece of fabric with decorated border pieces sewn on, or of several separately loomed pieces sewn together. These could be produced more quickly than the traditional single-loom shawls. See John Irwin, *The Kashmir Shawl* (London: Her Majesty's Stationery Office, 1973), 2. See also Frank Ames, *The Kashmir Shawl*

and Its Indo-French Influence (Woodbridge, Suffolk: Antique Collector's Club, 1997), 157.

2. See, for example, Annette B. Weiner and Jane Schneider, Introduction, *Cloth and Human Experience,* ed. Annette B. Weiner and Jane Schneider (Washington, DC: Smithsonian Institution Press, 1989), 15–16. See also Sherry Rehman and Naheed Jafri, *The Kashmiri Shawl: From Jamavar to Paisley* (Woodbridge, Suffolk: Antique Collectors' Club, 2006), 39–40.

3. Harriet Martineau, "Shawls," *Household Words* 5, no. 127 (August 1852): 552–53. An early example of this lesson's being taught also occurs in *Mansfield Park,* when Lady Bertram expresses a hope that her young nephew, who has just received a commission in the Navy, will be sent to the "East Indies" so that he can bring her back a shawl or two. See Jane Austen, *Mansfield Park,* vol. 3 of *Works,* ed. R. W. Chapman (Oxford: Oxford University Press, 1988), 305.

4. Elizabeth Gaskell, *Mary Barton* (Oxford: Oxford University Press, 1987), 3.

5. Gaskell, *Mary Barton,* 278.

6. Judith Walkowitz, *Prostitution and Victorian Society: Women, Class, and the State* (Cambridge: Cambridge University Press, 1980), 26.

7. Charlotte Brontë, *Villette* (1853; Oxford: Oxford University Press, 1990), 70 (emphasis in original).

8. Brontë, *Villette,* 86.

9. Brontë, *Villette,* 70.

10. See especially the first chapter in Andrew H. Miller's study *Novels Behind Glass: Commodity Culture and Victorian Narrative* (Cambridge: Cambridge University Press, 1995), 16–19, 30–31. For a discussion of servants and the moral dimensions of lower-class women's wearing of "finery," see Mariana Valverde, "The Love of Finery: Fashion and the Fallen Woman in Nineteenth-Century Discourse," *Victorian Studies* 32 (1989): 182–83.

11. For example, Lucy explains that she understood the significance of the events leading up to Miss Marchmont's death because she has witnessed three such deaths in her life (Brontë, *Villette,* 38); on arriving in Boue-Marine, she is confused by the foreign currency and overpays three times (Brontë, *Villette,* 51); in the course of the novel she arrives in three different cities—London, Boue-Marine, and Villette—alone, in the dark and rain; she is the governess of three children and the teacher of three forms; Mrs. Bretton's son has three distinct identities: Graham (the boy), Dr. John (the physician), and Isidore (Ginevra's lover); Lucy sees the nun three times; ascends to the attic three times; etc.

12. Brontë, *Villette,* 218.

13. For a sustained treatment of commodity fetishism in *Villette,* see Eva Badowska, "Choseville: Brontë's *Villette* and the Art of Bourgeois Interiority," *PMLA* 120 (2005): 1509–23.

14. Nicholas Dames, "The Clinical Novel: Phrenology and *Villette,*" *Novel* 29 (1996): 370; Brontë, *Villette,* 361.

15. Brontë, *Villette,* 369.

16. Brontë, *Villette*, 369–70.

17. Ellen Rosenman, "More Stories about Clothing and Furniture: Realism and Bad Commodities," in *Functions of Victorian Culture at the Present Time*, ed. Christine Krueger (Athens: Ohio University Press, 2002), 48.

18. Karl Marx and Friedrich Engels, "The Communist Manifesto," in *The Portable Karl Marx*, trans. S. Moore, ed. Eugene Kamenka (New York: Viking Penguin, 1983), 223.

19. Marx, *Grundrisse: Foundations of the Critique of Political Economy*, trans. Martin Nicolaus (New York: Penguin, 1993), 92. For critiques of this position, see Edmond Préteceille and Jean-Pierre Terrail, *Capitalism, Consumption, and Needs*, trans. Sarah Matthews (Oxford: Basil Blackwell, 1985), chapters 1–2; and Martyn J. Lee, *Consumer Culture Reborn: The Cultural Politics of Consumption* (London: Routledge, 1993), chapters 2–3.

20. Aileen Ribeiro, *The Art of Dress: Fashion in England and France, 1750–1820* (New Haven: Yale University Press, 1995), 125.

21. According to Ribeiro, attempts were even made to cultivate the goats in Scotland, but the texture of their coats changed in the new climate, and these efforts were abandoned.

22. For example, C. J. Hamilton, in *The Trade Relations between England and India (1600–1896)*, quotes a report on the external commerce of Bengal for 1804–5: "we should not be so sanguine as to expect that the demand for the piece-goods of India can ever be so great as formerly, since numerous and extensive manufactories have been recently established in the interior of France as well as in England. The weavers have there succeeded in imitating with so much exactness the fabrics of Bengal, particularly our coarse and middling assortments of muslins, that there is every reason to believe our trade in muslins of this description whether for the home or foreign markets must inevitably dwindle to nothing" (178).

23. Josephine's obsession with Kashmir shawls is well-known; she is said to have possessed hundreds of them and was frequently painted wearing them. See Ribeiro, *The Art of Dress*, especially chapter 3; see also Monique Lévi-Strauss, *The Cashmere Shawl*, trans. Sara Harris (New York: Harry N. Abrams, 1988), 16.

24. Robert Rosenblum, *Jean-Auguste-Dominique Ingres* (New York: Harry N. Abrams, 1986).

25. Georges Vigne, *Ingres*, trans. John Goodman (New York: Abbeville Press, 1995), 183.

26. Sarah Buie Pauley, "The Shawl: Its Context and Construction," in *The Kashmir Shawl: Yale University Art Gallery, February 12–April 6, 1975* (New Haven: Yale University Art Gallery, 1975), 8 (emphasis in original).

27. Brontë, *Villette*, 457.

28. While it is true that Said's *Orientalism* had not been published in 1975, Pauley (who later published under the surname Buie) reprinted an updated version of her article in 1996 with no modifications to this section. For a discussion of museum curators' relationship(s) to critiques of imperialism and Orientalism,

see Tim Barringer and Tom Flynn, eds., Introduction, *Colonialism and the Object: Empire, Material Culture, and the Museum* (London: Routledge, 1998). See also Nima Poovaya-Smith's article in the same volume, in which she affirms her "deep respect" for the work of Edward Said, Homi Bhabha, and Gayatri Chakravorty Spivak, but explains her need as a curator of a local museum in Bradford, England to "[set] it aside in order to let the [largely South Asian] public, the Bradford collections [of Indo-Pakistani art], and the exhibitions develop their own momentum" (Poovaya-Smith, "Keys to the Magic Kingdom," 112–13).

29. For example, in *Villette,* Brontë mentions "Bedreddin Hassan" (167), "the Slave of the Lamp" (209), "the Barmecide's loaf" (218), "the valley of Sindbad" (293), and "an Alnaschar dream" (441).

30. Romantic poetry and the works of Walter Scott are themselves freighted with *Arabian Nights* imagery. See Said's *Orientalism* on the failure of such mid-century novels as Benjamin Disraeli's *Tancred,* for which "the Oriental motif . . . was not principally a stylistic matter," as it seems to be for Brontë. *Tancred's* failure, Said argues, is predicated on Disraeli's "perhaps overdeveloped knowledge of Oriental politics and the British Establishment's network of interests," which force him "to confront a set of imposing resistances to his individual fantasy" (Said, *Orientalism,* 192–93).

31. Charlotte Brontë, *Jane Eyre* (1847; New York: Penguin, 2003), 208. For a discussion of such images in *Jane Eyre,* see Suvendrini Perera, *Reaches of Empire: The English Novel from Edgeworth to Dickens* (New York: Columbia University Press, 1991), chapter 4; see also Nandi Bhatia on the pressure Bengali men faced to adopt Western dress. Bhatia, "Fashioning Women in Colonial India," *Fashion Theory* 7 (2003): 327–44; for a compelling reading of Richard Burton's real-life "miming of nativeness," see Parama Roy, *Indian Traffic: Identities in Question in Colonial and Postcolonial India* (Berkeley: University of California Press, 1998), 27.

32. Brontë, *Villette,* 273.

33. Joan Copjec, *Read My Desire: Lacan Against the Historicists* (Cambridge: MIT Press, 1994), 106.

34. "Cashmere Shawls," *Once a Week* 12 (January 1865): 69.

35. Martineau, "Shawls," 553.

36. Marx, *Grundrisse,* 96.

37. Rebecca Wells Corrie, "The Paisley," in *The Kashmir Shawl: Yale University Art Gallery, February 12–April 6, 1975* (New Haven: Yale University Art Gallery, 1975), 24.

38. Corrie, "The Paisley," 47.

39. Corrie, "The Paisley," 26–27.

40. Corrie, "The Paisley," 26.

41. See Chitralekha Zutshi for an account of the East India Company's early concern to learn about Kashmiri shawl manufacturing. Zutshi, "'Designed for Eternity': Kashmiri Shawls, Empire, and Cultures of Production and Consumption in Mid-Victorian Britain," *Journal of British Studies* 48 (2009): 425.

42. Pamela Clabburn, "British Shawls in the Indian Style," in Frank Ames, *The Kashmir Shawl and Its Indo-French Influence* (Woodbridge, Suffolk: Antique Collector's Club, 1997), 244–48.

43. Clabburn, "British Shawls in the Indian Style," 245.

44. John Ruskin, *The Two Paths*, vols. 11–12 of *Complete Works* (New York: Thomas P. Crowell, 1909), 40. Ruskin mentions India and the Kashmir shawl in the first lecture of *The Two Paths*, titled "The Deteriorative Power of Conventional Art Over Nations." He expands his discussion of "savage nations" in the second lecture, "The Unity of Art," from which the above quotation is taken.

45. Irwin, *The Kashmir Shawl*, 25.

46. Sarah Buie, "The Kashmir Shawl," *Asian Art and Culture* 9 (1996): 41.

47. Ames, *The Kashmir Shawl and Its Indo-French Influence*, 19–20. *Shah tus* translates as "king of wools." According to the U.S. Customs service Web site, "United States federal laws and regulations restrict the importation, sale, purchase, and possession of Tibetan antelope parts and products. The Convention on International Trade in Endangered Species (CITES) of Wild Fauna and Flora regulates the trade in endangered species products, and since 1979, it has been illegal to import shahtoosh into the U.S. and many other countries. The Lacey Act also makes it a crime for anyone to import, export, transport, sell, receive, acquire, or buy wildlife or wildlife products that were taken, possessed, transported, or sold in violation of any law, treaty, or regulation of the U.S. or any state, tribal, or foreign law." Despite this, the shawls, which can cost up to $20,000 each, remain a status symbol for the wealthy.

48. William Thackeray, *Vanity Fair* (1848; Oxford: Oxford University Press, 1983), 63.

49. Buie, "The Kashmir Shawl," 43 (emphasis in original).

50. For a sustained reading of the role of the colonies in domestic English novels, see Edward Said, *Culture and Imperialism* (New York: Vintage, 1994).

51. "Cashmere Shawls," 68.

52. See Alison Adburgham, *Shops and Shopping, 1800–1914: Where, and in What Manner the Well-Dressed Englishwoman Bought Her Clothes* (London: George Allen and Unwin, 1964), 98–100, for a list of shawl purveyors. The surface explanation for women's demanding gifts of shawls would be that it was presumably less expensive to purchase them from a shawl broker abroad, and that they were more likely to be genuine.

53. See Buie, "The Kashmir Shawl," 39. In *Our Mutual Friend,* Bella Wilfer fantasizes about marrying an Indian prince "who wore Cashmere shawls all over himself, and diamonds and emeralds blazing in his turban" much as, the reader imagines, Bella herself would like to do (319).

54. Mary Elizabeth Braddon, *Lady Audley's Secret* (New York: Oxford, 1998), 374, 373.

55. Nupur Chaudhuri, "Shawls, Jewelry, Curry, and Rice in Victorian Britain," in *Western Women and Imperialism: Complicity and Resistance,* ed. Nupur

Chaudhuri and Margaret Strobel (Bloomington: Indiana University Press, 1992), 231. See also Bernard Cohn, "Cloth, Clothes, and Colonialism: India in the Nineteenth Century," in *Cloth and Human Experience,* ed. Annette B. Weiner and Jane Schneider (Washington, DC: Smithsonian Institution Press, 1989). Cohn argues that a notable exception to this practice could be found among the English "whose careers were spent up-country as British representatives in Muslim royal courts, where it was usual for some of them to live openly with Indian mistresses and to acknowledge their Indian children. These semi-Mughalized Europeans, although wearing European clothes in their public functions, affected Muslim dress in the privacy of their homes. The wearing of Indian dress in public functions by employees of the Company was officially banned in 1830" (310).

56. Margaret Oliphant, *Hester* (1883; New York: Penguin/Virago, 1984), 298.

57. A significant exception to this rule is Lizzie Eustace in Trollope's *The Eustace Diamonds,* which I discuss in chapter 3.

58. Charles White, *The Cashmere Shawl: An Eastern Fiction,* 3 vols. (London: Henry Colburn, 1840), vii.

59. White, *The Cashmere Shawl,* vii.

60. White, *The Cashmere Shawl,* viii.

61. White, *The Cashmere Shawl,* vii.

62. White, *The Cashmere Shawl,* ix–x (emphasis in original).

63. White, *The Cashmere Shawl,* xi.

64. White, *The Cashmere Shawl,* xi–xii.

65. Elizabeth Gaskell, *North and South* (New York: Penguin, 1995), 9.

66. Gaskell, *North and South,* 7.

67. Gaskell, *North and South,* 11, 25, 11.

68. Weiner and Schneider, Introduction, 4.

69. In a later example, George Eliot's *Mill on the Floss,* Mrs. Tulliver is horrified at the thought that her wedding linen, which she spun and embroidered herself, is to be sold at auction rather than passed down to her children. So must the unluckiest of the Dodson sisters give up the tangible markers of her ability to reproduce herself socially through her offspring. Eliot, *Mill on the Floss* (1860; New York: Signet, 1981), 215–17; for a discussion of social reproduction through the inheritance of clothing, see Martha C. Howell, "Fixing Movables: Gifts by Testament in Late Medieval Douai," *Past and Present* 150 (1996): 3–45; see also Ann Rosalind Jones and Peter Stallybrass, *Renaissance Clothing and the Materials of Memory* (Cambridge: Cambridge University Press, 2000).

70. Gaskell, *North and South,* 99.

71. Gaskell, *North and South,* 98, 100.

72. I am grateful to Radhika Jones for bringing this to my attention.

73. Gaskell, *North and South,* 139.

74. See chapter 1 of Gauri Viswanathan, *Outside the Fold: Conversion, Modernity, and Belief* (Princeton: Princeton University Press, 1998), for a reading of the literary projects of national cultural regeneration through religious con-

version and the related process she calls "attitudinal conversion," a "conversion of Anglican England to particular conceptions of future relationships with minority populations" (34); to suggest that Margaret Hale undergoes something like an attitudinal conversion toward industrialists is not to imply, however, that it is either possible or desirable to draw parallels between industrialists and religious minorities.

75. See, for example, Ramkrishna Mukherjee, *The Rise and Fall of the East India Company: A Sociological Appraisal* (New York: Monthly Review Press, 1974), chapter 5, for a discussion of the "ruination of artisans" and the forcible sale of British goods; see also C. A. Bayly, "The Origins of Swadeshi (Home Industry): Cloth and Indian Society, 1700–1930," in *The Social Life of Things: Commodities in Cultural Perspective* (Cambridge: Cambridge University Press, 1986). Bayly notes, "After 1905, the import of British-made cloth into India and the ensuing destruction of Indian handicraft production became the key theme of Indian nationalism" (285). Bayly, unlike Mukherjee, sees the takeover of the Indian textile market largely in terms of changing tastes and economic factors (302–8). He argues that as in the case of European desire for Indian shawls, the quality of the products produced the desire to own them, but acknowledges the role of the creation of a "colonial elite" who felt impelled to imitate Western dress in the workplace and therefore needed English textiles in order to dress the part.

76. In *Imagined Communities,* Benedict Anderson categorizes the conquest of India as belonging to a "prenational age" thus: " 'India' only became 'British' twenty years after Victoria's accession to the throne. In other words, until after the 1857 Mutiny, 'India' was ruled by a commercial enterprise—not by a state, and certainly not by a nation-state" (90).

77. D. N. Dhar, *Socio-Economic History of Kashmir Peasantry* (Srinaghar, Kashmir: Centre for Kashmir Studies, 1989), appendix J. See also Irwin, *The Kashmir Shawl,* 24.

78. "Shawls," 552. This is not to say that shawls were not important to South Asian royalty, only that the *Household Words* article, by exaggerating the time scale ("thousands of years"), contributes to the hypostasizing of what were in fact diverse and historically contingent practices (552). See Rehman and Jaffri, *The Kashmiri Shawl,* 47–57, for more on nineteenth-century court practices.

79. Adrienne Munich, *Queen Victoria's Secrets* (New York: Columbia University Press, 1996), 147.

80. Irwin, *The Kashmir Shawl,* 25.

81. "Cashmere Shawls," 68.

82. See Patrick Brantlinger, *Rule of Darkness: British Literature and Imperialism, 1830–1914* (Ithaca: Cornell University Press, 1988). See especially chapter 7, "The Well at Cawnpore: Literary Representations of the Mutiny of 1857." See also Sangeeta Ray, *En-Gendering India: Woman and Nation in Colonial and Postcolonial Narratives* (Durham: Duke University Press, 2000). See especially chapter 2, "Woman as 'Suttee': The Construction of India in Three Victorian Narratives."

83. Manohar Lal Kapur, *Social and Economic History of Jammu and Kashmir State, 1885–1923 A.D.* (New Delhi: Anmol, 1992), 275–77.

84. "An Extinct Art," *Magazine of Art* 25 (1901): 452.

85. N. N. Raina, *Kashmir Politics and Imperialist Manoeuvres, 1846–1980* (New Delhi: Patriot, 1988), 21.

86. Oliphant, *Hester,* 231, 235.

87. Oscar Wilde, *The Importance of Being Earnest and Other Plays* (Oxford: Oxford University Press, 1998), 4.1.104, 4.1.105–6.

CHAPTER 2

1. Arthur Silver, *Manchester Men and Indian Cotton, 1847–1872* (Manchester: Manchester University Press, 1966), 26.

2. The article "Indian Cotton and Its Supply," which appeared in *Cornhill* in 1862, when the American Civil War was well under way, is a good example of the argument for "reforming" the Indian cotton industry so that it might supply English mills with raw material. See also the 1861 article "The Cotton Manufacture" in the *Westminster Review.*

3. John Keay, *The Honourable Company: A History of the English East India Company* (London: HarperCollins, 1991), 98–99.

4. For an overview of the eighteenth-century Bengal trade, see N. K. Sinha, *Economic History of Bengal,* 3 vols. (Calcutta: Firma K. L. Mukhopadhyay, 1956–70). See especially volume 1, chapters 6 and 8.

5. K. N. Chaudhuri, *The Trading World of Asia and the English East India Company* (New York: Cambridge University Press, 1978), 282.

6. Beverly Lemire, *Fashion's Favourite: The Cotton Trade and the Consumer in Britain, 1660–1800* (Oxford: Oxford University Press, 1991), 16–17.

7. Lemire, *Fashion's Favourite,* 20.

8. Jones and Stallybrass, *Renaissance Clothing,* 66.

9. Lemire, *Fashion's Favourite,* 21.

10. Lemire, *Fashion's Favourite,* 24–25.

11. Quoted in Lemire, *Fashion's Favourite,* 31.

12. For a discussion of how the dismantling of the Indian textile industries has been narrativized, see Bipan Chandra, *Essays on Colonialism* (Hyderabad: Orient Longman, 1999). See especially his essay "Reinterpretation of Nineteenth-Century Indian Economic History." See also Immanuel Wallerstein, *The Modern World-System III: The Second Era of Great Expansion of the Capitalist World-Economy, 1730–1840s* (San Diego: Academic Press, 1989), 149–50; and Sinha, *Economic History of Bengal,* vol. 3, especially chapter 1. For a reading of what he calls "transition narratives," see Dipesh Chakrabarty, *Provincializing Europe: Postcolonial Thought and Historical Difference* (Princeton: Princeton University Press, 2000), especially chapter 1.

13. For example, Elaine Freedgood has demonstrated that the calico curtains

in *Mary Barton* at once "indicate domesticity, and hence orderly relations between men and women, children and adults, home and world" and gesture at "the history of the deindustrialization of the Indian textile manufacture, and the rise to dominance of British cotton production" (57). See Freedgood, *The Ideas in Things: Fugitive Meaning in the Victorian Novel* (Chicago: University of Chicago Press, 2006), chapter 2.

14. This article appears in the same number as an installment of Margaret Oliphant's *Miss Marjoribanks,* which I discuss later in this chapter.

15. Mozley, "Dress," *Blackwood's Magazine* 57 (April 1865): 426.

16. Mozley, "Dress," 431.

17. Suzanne Keen, "Quaker Dress, Sexuality, and the Domestication of Reform in the Victorian Novel," *Victorian Literature and Culture* 30 (2002): 212.

18. Elizabeth Gaskell, *Wives and Daughters* (New York: Penguin, 2001), 5.

19. Gaskell, *Wives and Daughters,* 5.

20. Franco Moretti, *The Way of the World: The Bildungsroman in European Culture* (London: Verso, 2000), 15 (emphasis in original). Moretti explains that for modern bourgeois society to function, the "free individual" must "*internalize* [social norms] and fuse external compulsion and internal impulses into a new unity until the former is no longer distinguishable from the latter" (16; emphasis in original).

21. Gaskell, *Wives and Daughters,* 6.

22. Gaskell, *Wives and Daughters,* 35.

23. Jones and Stallybrass, *Renaissance Clothing,* 134.

24. Gaskell, *Wives and Daughters,* 5.

25. Gaskell, *Wives and Daughters,* 5.

26. Gaskell, *Wives and Daughters,* 16

27. Gaskell, *Wives and Daughters,* 141.

28. Gaskell, *Wives and Daughters,* 140. Judith Walkowitz quotes the journalist James Greenwood as describing the dress of prostitutes in a similar manner; the typical prostitute, he writes, wears "a fashionably made skirt and jacket of some cheap and flashy material and nothing besides in the way of under-garments but a few tattered rags that a professional beggar would despise" (Greenwood, *In Strange Company,* 132; quoted in Walkowitz, *Prostitution and Victorian Society: Women, Class, and the State* [Cambridge: Cambridge University Press, 1980], 26).

29. Gaskell, *Wives and Daughters,* 428.

30. Gaskell, *Wives and Daughters,* 63. The novel takes place "before the passing of the Reform Bill" (36).

31. Gaskell, *Wives and Daughters,* 63.

32. Gaskell, *Wives and Daughters,* 154–55.

33. Gaskell, *Wives and Daughters,* 437.

34. Gaskell, *Wives and Daughters,* 474.

35. Gaskell, *Wives and Daughters,* 131.

36. Gaskell, *Wives and Daughters,* 22, 159.

37. Gaskell, *Wives and Daughters,* 153.

38. Gaskell, *Wives and Daughters,* 152.

39. Margaret Oliphant, *Miss Marjoribanks* (New York: Penguin, 1998), 53.

40. Elisabeth Jay, Introduction, *Miss Marjoribanks,* by Margaret Oliphant (New York: Penguin, 1998), xxix.

41. Jay, Introduction, *Miss Marjoribanks,* xxvi.

42. Gaskell, *Wives and Daughters,* 158.

43. Oliphant, *Miss Marjoribanks,* 85.

44. Oliphant, *Miss Marjoribanks,* 21.

45. Joseph H. O'Mealy, "Mrs. Oliphant, *Miss Marjoribanks* (1866), and the Victorian Canon," in *The New Nineteenth Century: Feminist Readings of Underread Victorian Novels,* ed. Barbara Leah Harmon and Susan Meyer (New York: Garland, 1996), 72–73.

46. O'Mealy, "Mrs. Oliphant, *Miss Marjoribanks* (1866), and the Victorian Canon," 74.

47. Oliphant, *Miss Marjoribanks,* 495.

48. It could be argued that in *North and South,* part of Thornton's outrage at Margaret Hale after he mistakes her brother for a lover is that she *appears* so respectable: "how could one so pure have stooped from her decorous and noble manner of bearing!" (273).

49. Elizabeth Gaskell, *Ruth* (New York: Penguin, 2004), 14.

50. Gaskell, *Ruth,* 61.

51. Gaskell, *Ruth,* 133.

52. Gaskell, *Ruth,* 62.

53. Gaskell, *Ruth,* 133.

54. Gaskell, *Ruth,* 40.

55. Gaskell, *Ruth,* 39.

56. Silver, *Manchester Men,* 4. Silver also writes, for example, that between 1815 and 1875, cotton generally provided between 30 and 45 percent of England's exports (1).

57. "Cotton," *Chambers's Journal* 19 (1863): 136–37.

58. "Cotton," *Chambers's Journal,* 137.

59. "Cotton," *Chambers's Journal,* 137.

60. "Cotton," *Chambers's Journal,* 136.

61. "The Cotton Fields of India," *Dublin University Magazine* 49 (1857): 678.

62. Watson's book was printed for the India Office in 1866 (Philip Meadows Taylor, "Indian Costumes and Textile Fabrics," *Edinburgh Review* 126 [July 1867]: 125). It was conceived as an introduction to and analysis of an eighteen-volume collection of specimens of Indian textiles and threads, compiled by Watson, "which have been distributed to manufacturing cities in Great Britain" (quoted in Taylor, "Indian Costumes," 138). Watson writes, "The 700 specimens . . . show what the people of India affect, and deem suitable, in the way of textile fabrics;

and if the supply of these is to come from Great Britain, they must be imitated there" (138).

63. Taylor, "Indian Costumes," 125.

64. Taylor, "Indian Costumes," 147.

65. For example, in the "Accessions and Notes" section of the 1925 *Metropolitan Museum of Art Bulletin,* remarks on the rarity of a recently acquired piece of Belgian lace, made in 1853 for Henriette Marie, Archduchess of Austria, at the time of her marriage to King Leopold II of Belgium, read in part, "Today, Belgium's younger lace-makers are no longer willing to risk eyesight in the perfection of difficult technique" (87). Similarly, a 1905 essay by Emily Leland Harrison titled "Ancient Lace," published in the *Bulletin of the Pennsylvania Museum,* notes that Belgian lace was produced "often at cost of eyesight and even of life" (1905, 28).

66. "Cotton," *Chambers's Journal,* 136, 137.

67. In *Pendennis* (1850), the "pretty bit of muslin" with whom Pen has been seen at Vauxhall is Fanny Bolton, his housekeeper's daughter. This exchange, and the social scrutiny it implies, marks the point at which Pen's extremely short-lived passion for her begins to wane. Fanny is, if not as designing as Pen's other love-interests, at least persistent, but she is vanquished by Pen's mother, Helen. William Thackeray, *The History of Pendennis* (Oxford: Oxford World's Classics, 1994), 636.

68. For example, Stephen Blackpool in *Hard Times* is a power-loom weaver; cotton mills also feature in Gaskell's *North and South* and *Mary Barton,* as well as Frances Trollope's 1840 novel *Michael Armstrong, Factory Boy.*

69. For a thorough treatment of the novels' similarities, see Michael Wheeler, "Two Tales of Manchester Life," *Gaskell Society Journal* 3 (1989): 6–28.

70. Elizabeth Stone, *William Langshawe, The Cotton Lord* (London: Richard Bentley, 1842), 1:124.

71. Stone, *William Langshawe,* 1:16. It is perhaps worth mentioning here that, as Graham Law observes, "it is indeed to the textile industry of Lancashire in the 1840s that we can trace the origin of Marxist thought" (Law, "Industrial Designs: Form and Function in the 'Condition-of-England' Novel," in *Corresponding Powers: Studies in Honor of Professor Hisaaki Yamanouchi,* ed. George Hughes [Cambridge: D. S. Brewer, 1997], 127).

72. Marx, *Capital,* vol. 1, trans. Ben Fowkes (New York: Vintage, 1977), 247.

73. See, for example, the descriptions of rooms and meals (1:37–42, 1:137–43, 1:185) and also Stone's defense of the cotton masters (1:174–75; especially 1:189–98).

74. Marx, *Capital,* 1:248.

75. Stone, *William Langshawe,* 1:14.

76. Stone, *William Langshawe,* 1:168.

77. Stone, *William Langshawe,* 1:169.

78. Stone, *William Langshawe,* 1:175.

79. Law, "Industrial Designs," 126.

80. Law, "Industrial Designs," 127.

81. Law, "Industrial Designs," 128.

82. Rosemarie Bodenheimer, *The Politics of Story in Victorian Social Fiction* (Ithaca: Cornell University Press, 1988), 76.

83. Bodenheimer, *The Politics of Story,* 74.

84. Stone, *William Langshawe,* 1:64–66 (emphasis in original).

85. Stone, *William Langshawe,* 2:163. For a reading of the political implications of this passage, see Law, "Industrial Designs," 132–34. "Slaves, o'erworn with toil" appears to be a slight misquotation of Emma Roberts's 1826 poem "Constance: A Tale," which is set in India.

86. Stone, *William Langshawe,* 1:189.

87. Stone, *William Langshawe,* 2:108.

88. Stone, *William Langshawe,* 1:183 (emphasis in original).

89. Benjamin Disraeli, *Sybil, or the Two Nations* (Oxford: Oxford University Press, 1998), 76.

90. For more, see Michael Flavin, *Disraeli: The Novel as Political Discourse* (Brighton: Sussex Academic Press, 2005).

91. Disraeli, *Sybil,* 97.

92. Disraeli, *Sybil,* 78.

93. Harnetty, *Imperialism and Free Trade: Lancashire and India in the Mid-Nineteenth Century* (Vancouver: University of British Columbia Press, 1972), 7.

94. See Silver, *Manchester Men,* chapters 1–3.

95. Harnetty, *Imperialism and Free Trade,* 4.

96. See Janice Helland, "'Caprices of Fashion': Handmade Lace in Ireland, 1883–1907" (*Textile History* 39 [2008]), in which she relates how nineteenth-century lace carried contradictory associations of luxury and exploitation. See also Elaine Freedgood, "'Fine Fingers': Victorian Handmade Lace and Utopian Consumption," *Victorian Studies* 45 (2003).

97. Charlotte Yonge, *The Clever Woman of the Family* (New York: Penguin/Virago, 1986), 337.

98. Yonge, *Clever Woman,* 53.

99. Yonge, *Clever Woman,* 82, 106.

100. Yonge, *Clever Woman,* 176.

101. Yonge, *Clever Woman,* 181. The story of the siege of Lucknow and the subsequent evacuation of the British women who were confined to the Residency compound was well-known in part because several of the women subsequently published their diaries. For a reading of these diaries, see Alison Blunt, "'The Flight from Lucknow': British Women Travelling and Writing Home, 1857–8," in *Writes of Passage: Reading Travel Writing,* ed. James Duncan and Derek Gregory (London: Routledge, 1999).

102. Yonge, *Clever Woman,* 197.

103. Yonge, *Clever Woman,* 204.

104. Yonge, *Clever Woman,* 204.

105. Yonge, *Clever Woman,* 219.

106. Yonge, *Clever Woman,* 228.

107. Perhaps more strikingly, Maria Hatherton is figured as an Indian man. Indian women virtually never appear in domestic Victorian fiction, although ayahs occasionally make appearances in children's literature, particularly Christian children's literature. For more on the sexualized conflation of English women with Indian "mutineers," see Terri A. Hasseler, "Mr. Punch's Crinoline Anxiety: The Indian Rebellion and the Rhetoric of Dress," in *Comedy, Fantasy, and Colonialism,* ed. Graeme Harper (London: Continuum, 2002), 117–39.

108. Yonge, *Clever Woman,* 339.

109. Yonge, *Clever Woman,* 176.

110. Yonge, *Clever Woman,* 304–5.

CHAPTER 3

1. T. M. Babu, *Diamonds in India* (Bangalore: Geological Society of India, 1998), 81–82.

2. The Hope Diamond was stolen during the French Revolution and made its way to London, where it was recut. It was taken then back to France, where it was owned by the jeweler Pierre Cartier, and finally removed to the United States where it was owned by *Washington Post* heiress Evalyn Walsh McLean. She sold it to Harry Winston, who donated the diamond to the Smithsonian Institution, where it currently resides in the Museum of Natural History. It is popularly believed to carry a curse. See George E. Harlow, "The World's Great Diamonds," in *The Nature of Diamonds,* ed. Harlow (Cambridge: Cambridge University Press, 1998), 105.

3. Alfred A. Levinson, "Diamond Sources and Their Discovery," in *The Nature of Diamonds,* ed. Harlow, 78.

4. Levinson, "Diamond Sources and Their Discovery," 75.

5. For more on paintings of the fall of Srirangapatna, see Mildred Archer, *Tippoo's Tiger* (London: H.M. Stationery Office, 1959), plates 14–18, and Hermione de Almeida and George H. Gilpin, *Indian Renaissance: British Romantic Art and the Prospect of India* (Aldershot: Ashgate, 2006), 159–66.

6. Molly Youngkin, " 'Into the Woof, A Little Thibet Wool': Orientalism and Representing 'Reality' in Walter Scott's *The Surgeon's Daughter,*" *Scottish Studies Review* 3 (2002): 33.

7. Walter Scott, *The Surgeon's Daughter,* Waverley novels, vol. 20, *Chronicles of the Canongate,* first series (Boston: Sanborn, Carter and Bazin, 1855), ix.

8. Scott, Introduction, *The Surgeon's Daughter,* n.p.

9. Scott, *Surgeon's Daughter,* 12.

10. Scott, *Surgeon's Daughter,* 13.

11. Scott, *Surgeon's Daughter,* 14.

12. Scott, *Surgeon's Daughter,* 192–93.

13. In their introduction to *The Surgeon's Daughter,* the editors of the Walter Scott digital collection at the University of Edinburgh note, "It has not to date been

established whether Train's anecdote derives from a true story." *Walter Scott Digital Archive,* Edinburgh University, http://www.walterscott.lib.ed.ac.uk/works/novels/ daughter.html. See also Claire Lamont's Historical Note to *The Surgeon's Daughter,* especially 357, in her Penguin edition of the *Chronicles* (London, 2003).

14. Scott, *Surgeon's Daughter,* viii.

15. Scott, *Surgeon's Daughter,* 72.

16. Scott, *Surgeon's Daughter,* 158.

17. Scott, *Surgeon's Daughter,* 74.

18. Scott, *Surgeon's Daughter,* 163.

19. Scott, *Surgeon's Daughter,* 185–86.

20. Andrew Lincoln, *Walter Scott and Modernity* (Edinburgh: Edinburgh University Press, 2007), 94.

21. In his reading of *The Surgeon's Daughter,* Upamanyu Pablo Mukherjee gives a persuasive account of the competing ideas about India and imperialism that inform Scott's narrative. See *Crime and Empire: The Colony in Nineteenth-Century Fictions of Crime* (Oxford: Oxford University Press, 2003), 66–71. For more on the historical context in which Scott was writing, see Saree Makdisi, *Romantic Imperialism: Universal Empire and the Culture of Modernity* (Cambridge: Cambridge University Press, 1998), chapter 5.

22. See Henry James Wye Milley, "The Eustace Diamonds and the Moonstone," *Studies in Philology* 36 (1939): 651–63.

23. Anthony Trollope, *Autobiography* (London: Penguin, 1996), 226–27. For more on Trollope and realism, see David Skilton, *Anthony Trollope and His Contemporaries: A Study in the Theory and Conventions of Mid-Victorian Fiction* (New York: St. Martin's, 1996), 149–52.

24. Lord Wellesley (later the Duke of Wellington) described the siege in a letter: "Scarcely a house in the town was left unplundered, and I understand that in camp jewels of the greatest value, bars of gold, &c. &c. have been offered for sale in the bazaars of the army by our soldiers, sepoys, and followers." Arthur Wellesley, Duke of Wellington, *Supplementary Despatches and Memoranda of Field Marshal Arthur Duke of Wellington, K.G.,* vol. 1 (London: John Murray, 1858), 212.

25. These include Andrew Miller's reading of *The Eustace Diamonds* in *Novels Behind Glass: Commodity Culture and Victorian Narrative* (Cambridge: Cambridge University Press, 1995) and, more recently, Christoph Lindner's in *Fictions of Commodity Culture* (Aldershot, Hampshire: Ashgate, 2003) and John Plotz's in *Portable Property: Victorian Culture on the Move* (Princeton: Princeton University Press, 2008).

26. See, for example, Tamar Heller, *Dead Secrets: Wilkie Collins and the Female Gothic* (New Haven: Yale University Press, 1992); Ian Duncan, "*The Moonstone,* the Victorian Novel, and Imperialist Panic," *MLQ* 55, no. 3 (fall 1994): 297–319; and Jaya Mehta, "English Romance; Indian Violence," *Centennial Review* 39 (fall 1995): 611–57.

27. The Moonstone is difficult to define in part because it exemplifies Arjun

Appadurai's claim that the meaning of things must be located *in their movement;* possessed by the Brahmins, the diamond is a sacred relic; by Rachel, it is an ornament; by Franklin Blake, a commodity, something to be sold for profit. See Appadurai's introduction to his edited collection *The Social Life of Things.* For more on the social life of objects, see Victoria de Grazia's introduction to *The Sex of Things: Gender and Consumption in Historical Perspective,* ed. Victoria de Grazia with Ellen Furlough (Berkeley: University of California Press, 1996), and Mary Douglas and Baron Isherwood, *The World of Goods: Toward an Anthropology of Consumption* (New York: W. W. Norton, 1979).

28. When G. H. Lewes, the original editor, resigned in November 1866, Trollope hired Morley to replace him. Trollope had misgivings, however, and his relationship with Morley was vexed at times. See N. John Hall, ed., *The Letters of Anthony Trollope,* 2 vols. (Stanford: Stanford University Press, 1983), 354, 364, and especially 381, where Trollope writes (in June 1867), "I do not specially dislike Morley, but I do not care for his style of work." See also Trollope's *Autobiography,* 194. After a distinguished career as a radical journalist and member of Parliament, Morley became secretary of state for India in 1905, at which time he argued that India was neither "capable of a complete system of responsible government" nor "fitted for a democratic constitution" (*Dictionary of National Biography*).

29. See Charles Dickens, *Oliver Twist* (New York: Penguin, 2003), chapter 38; Wilkie Collins, *Hide and Seek* (New York: Oxford, 1999); George Eliot, *Felix Holt: The Radical* (New York: Penguin, 1995). For more on the semiotics of jewelry, see Marcia Pointon, "Intriguing Jewellery: Royal Bodies and Luxurious Consumption," *Textual Practice* 11 (1997): 495.

30. Elizabeth Gaskell, *Wives and Daughters* (New York: Penguin, 2001), 290–91.

31. Elizabeth Gaskell, *Cranford* (New York: Penguin, 1986), 207–8.

32. Rudyard Kipling, *The Jungle Books* (New York: Penguin, 1989), 262–63.

33. Kipling, *The Jungle Books,* 263.

34. Anne McClintock, *Imperial Leather: Race, Gender, and Sexuality in the Colonial Contest* (New York: Routledge, 1995), 247–48.

35. For a sustained consideration of the troping of imperialism as rape, see Jenny Sharpe, *Allegories of Empire: The Figure of Woman in the Colonial Text* (Minneapolis: University of Minnesota Press, 1993), especially chapter 6.

36. Franco Moretti, *Atlas of the European Novel, 1800–1900* (London: Verso, 1998), 62.

37. Arthur Conan Doyle, *The Complete Sherlock Holmes,* vol. 1 (Garden City, NY: Doubleday, 1960), 249. Recounting the history of Indian diamonds in *Traditional Jewelry of India* (New York: Harry N. Abrams, 1997), Oppi Untracht seems to echo Holmes: "The drive to possess diamonds has resulted in more intrigue, scandal, treachery, violence, and prolonged or sudden death . . . than any imaginative fiction writer could invent" (312).

38. Wilkie Collins, *The Moonstone* (Oxford: World's Classics, 1982), 36.

39. Anthony Trollope, *The Eustace Diamonds* (Oxford: Oxford University Press, 1983), I.100.

40. For a reading of the trajectory of the novel's criminal activity, see D. A. Miller, *The Novel and the Police* (Berkeley: University of California Press, 1988), 11–16.

41. See, for example, Leonore Davidoff and Catherine Hall, *Family Fortunes: Men and Women of the Middle Class, 1780–1850* (London: Hutchinson, 1987), and Nancy Armstrong, *Desire and Domestic Fiction: A Political History of the Novel* (New York: Oxford University Press, 1987), especially chapter 2, "The Rise of the Domestic Woman."

42. Priscilla L. Walton, *Patriarchal Desire and Victorian Discourse: A Lacanian Reading of Anthony Trollope's Palliser Novels* (Toronto: University of Toronto Press, 1995), 68 (emphasis in original).

43. Like the cousin-pairs of Lizzie and Frank, and Rachel and Franklin in *The Moonstone,* Queen Victoria herself had differences over diamonds with her cousin, George V, the King of Hanover, who claimed he had been bequeathed certain of the English crown jewels by Queen Charlotte. See Victoria, *The Letters of Queen Victoria,* vol. 1, ed. Arthur Christopher Benson and Viscount Esher (New York: Longmans, Green), 550. For more on Charlotte and her gems, see Pointon, "Intriguing Jewellery."

44. D. A. Miller, *Jane Austen, or, the Secret of Style* (Princeton: Princeton University Press, 2003), 11 (emphasis in original).

45. A. O. J. Cockshut, *Anthony Trollope: A Critical Study* (London: Collins, 1955), 183.

46. In his edition of Trollope's *Eustace Diamonds* (Oxford: Oxford University Press, 1983), McCormack mentions *Othello, Romeo and Juliet,* and *Love's Labour's Lost* as obvious sources (383–85), although he does not mention that in the latter, the romance between the King of Navarre and the Princess of France is deferred at the play's end despite the fact that he has given her diamonds as a pledge. *Cymbeline* lurks in the background of *The Eustace Diamonds* as well, as its plot turns on the question of whether Imogen is as pure as her diamond.

47. William Cohen, "Trollope's Trollop," *Novel* 28 (1995): 235–56.

48. John Halperin, "The Eustace Diamonds and Politics," in *Anthony Trollope,* ed. Tony Bareham (London: Vision Press, 1980), 152.

49. The dispute is recorded in the Parliamentary Papers for 1866–67.

50. The state of Mysore was renamed Karnataka in 1959. Indian proper names tend to have been transliterated differently at different moments; the Maharajah is referred to in the Parliamentary Papers as Raj Wudayer Bahadoor, and in the 1799 Subsidiary Treaty as "Kishna [*sic*] Rajah Oodiaver Bahadoor." In the text, I follow the spelling used by H. V. Sreenivasa Murthy and R. Ramakrishnan in *A History of Karnataka (From the Earliest Times to the Present Day)* (New Delhi: S. Chand and Company, 1977).

51. See, for example, McCormack, Introduction, *The Eustace Diamonds,*

xvi–xxi, which section he concludes by asserting that "what we have done is to burst the balloon which is inflated by vaporous opinions as to the non-political nature of *The Eustace Diamonds* by placing it in a historically alert series of comparisons to other narratives" (xx).

52. Murthy and Ramakrishnan, *Brief History of Karnataka,* 306–9.

53. Murthy and Ramakrishnan, *Brief History of Karnataka,* 311.

54. A *lakh* is a unit of 100,000.

55. Adrian Sever, ed., *Documents and Speeches on the Indian Princely States,* vol. 1 (Delhi: B. R. Publishing, 1985), 95–97.

56. *Dictionary of National Biography on CD-ROM,* Version 1.0., s.v. "Cubbon, Sir Mark 1784–1861" (Oxford: Oxford University Press, 1995).

57. Parliamentary Papers (1866), 1–2.

58. Parliamentary Papers (1866), 3.

59. The *OED*'s first citation for the use of "jewels in the crown" to denote England's colonies is 1901. Jenny Sharpe, however, quotes Marianne Postans (also known as Marianne Young) from 1839: "[India] is spoken of, indeed, as 'the brightest jewel in the British crown.'" *Western India in 1838,* 2:283, quoted in Sharpe, *Allegories of Empire,* 149.

60. Bernard S. Cohn, "Cloth, Clothes, and Colonialism: India in the Nineteenth Century," in *Cloth and Human Experience,* ed. Annette B. Weiner and Jane Schneider (Washington, DC: Smithsonian Institution Press, 1989), 319.

61. The reference to "even" a natural-born heir is significant in that it refers to the fact that under the governor-generalship of Dalhousie, the British ceased to recognize adopted heirs and claimed as British territory princely states in which the ruler died without male issue. Traditionally, princes without male issue would adopt a son, usually the child of a close relative, with the understanding that the child would inherit the throne. This was the case with Krishnaraja, who hoped to see his adopted son Chamarajah inherit his title as well as the right to rule.

62. The term *princely state* is problematic in that, as the Mysore case demonstrates, differentiating these variously autonomous states from British territory proper is tricky at best; furthermore, the word *prince* suggests a constellation of meanings not necessarily carried by *rajah*. Spivak makes this point regarding the translation of *rani* as *queen* (*A Critique of Postcolonial Reason,* 201 n. 9).

CHAPTER 4

1. Roland Barthes, *Mythologies,* trans. Annette Lavers (New York: Hill and Wang, 1972), 58.

2. Karl Marx, "Whose Atrocities?" Marxists Internet Archive, http://www.marxists.org/archive/marx/works/1857/04/10.htm. This article, first published in the *New York Daily Tribune* on April 10, 1857, was written in response to British hostilities in Canton, China.

3. Karl Marx, *Capital,* vol. 1, trans. Ben Fowkes (New York: Vintage, 1977), 164–65.

4. Anne McClintock, *Imperial Leather: Race, Gender, and Sexuality in the Colonial Contest* (New York: Routledge, 1995), 170.

5. Mary Smith comes up with the idea of Matty's selling tea in chapter 14, titled "Friends in Need." In the very next chapter, "A Happy Return," Matty is briefly seen in business before her brother Peter appears and her need to engage in commerce is obviated.

6. An exception is Disraeli's *Sybil,* in which the working-class activist Devilsdust inveighs against consuming "exciseable articles" (133), including tea.

7. See Julie Fromer's *A Necessary Luxury: Tea in Victorian England* (Athens: Ohio University Press, 2008), chapter 1, for a narrative of the move from Chinese to Indian tea.

8. James Walvin, *Fruits of Empire: Exotic Produce and British Taste, 1660–1800* (New York: New York University Press, 1997), 21–22. Philip Lawson makes much the same point in his article "Women and the Empire of Tea: Image and Counterimage in Hanoverian England," which appears in *A Taste for Empire and Glory: Studies in British Overseas Expansion, 1660–1800* (Aldershot: Variorum/Ashgate, 1997). See also, in the same volume, "Tea, Vice, and the English State, 1660–1784."

9. "Indian Teas and Chinese Travellers," *Fraser's Magazine* 47 (January 1853): 88.

10. Marx, "Revolution in China and in Europe," *Surveys from Exile,* 330.

11. Dutta, *Cha Garam!* 15.

12. For a history of tea dealing, see William H. Ukers, *All About Tea,* vol. 2 (New York: Tea and Coffee Trade Journal Company, 1935), 129–31.

13. Denys Forrest, *Tea for the British: The Social and Economic History of a Famous Trade* (London: Chatto and Windus, 1973), 30. Forrest argues that the low prices of smuggled tea often reflected the fact that it was highly adulterated, usually with sloe leaves or elder buds (55). Coffee was thus less popular with smugglers, as the beans could not be adulterated until they were ground.

14. For discussions of tea's role in the temperance movement, see Beth Kowaleski-Wallace, "Tea, Gender, and Domesticity in Eighteenth-Century England," *Studies in Eighteenth-Century Culture* 23 (1994): 131–45. See also Forrest, 87–88, and Fromer, *A Necessary Luxury,* 30.

15. Dutta, *Cha Garam!* 79.

16. John Galt, *Annals of the Parish* (Edinburgh: Mercat, 1994), 11.

17. Galt, *Annals of the Parish,* 12.

18. Galt, *Annals of the Parish,* 99.

19. Kowaleski-Wallace, "Tea, Gender, and Domesticity," 135.

20. Kowaleski-Wallace, "Tea, Gender, and Domesticity," 139–40.

21. Annabella Plumptre, *Domestic Management; or, The Healthful Cookery-Book.* Quoted in Eric Quayle, *Old Cook Books: An Illustrated History* (New York: Brandywine-E. P. Dutton, 1978), 126–27.

22. Plumptre, quoted in Quayle, *Old Cook Books,* 127.

23. Jane Austen, *Sanditon,* in *Works,* vol. 6, *Minor Works,* ed. R. W. Chapman (Oxford: Oxford University Press, 1988), 418.

24. Mrs. Beeton, *Mrs. Beeton's Book of Household Management* (London: S. O. Beeton, 1861), 899.

25. In *Cranford,* which is set in the 1830s, Mary Smith expresses amusement at Matty's old-fashioned aversion to green tea (174, 202). In Dickens's *Our Mutual Friend* (Oxford: Oxford World's Classics, 1989), Mr. Fledgeby, who like Veneering and Podsnap speaks only in commonplaces and clichés and is known as "Fascination Fledgeby" "in facetious homage to the smallness of his talk" (261), hands coffee to Georgiana Podsnap with "the original embellishment of informing [her] that green tea was considered bad for the nerves" (264). See Fromer, *A Necessary Luxury,* 39–40, for a discussion of the racialization of Chinese tea.

26. Bramah Tea and Coffee Museum, *Guide and Souvenir Book* (London: Bramah Tea and Coffee Museum, 1997), 13.

27. See Walvin, *Fruits of Empire,* 22–23.

28. Forrest, *Tea for the British,* 285.

29. For histories of the annexation of Assam and the development of the Indian tea industry, see, in addition to Goswami, K. T. Achaya, *The Food Industries of British India* (Delhi: Oxford University Press, 1994), chapter 6; H. K. Barpujari, both *Assam in the Days of the Company (1826–1858)* (Gauhati, Assam: Spectrum, 1980) and especially his *Comprehensive History of Assam,* vol. 5, *Modern Period: Yandabo to Diarchy, 1826–1919 A.D.* (Guwahati: Publication Board Assam, 1990), chapter 3; and Amalendu Guha, "Colonisation of Assam: Second Phase, 1840–1859," *Indian Economic and Social History Review* 4 (1967): 289–318, and especially *Planter-Raj to Swaraj: Freedom Struggle and Electoral Politics in Assam, 1826–1947* (New Delhi: Indian Council of Historical Research, 1977). For the text of the Treaty of Yandaboo (or Yandabo), under which Assam was annexed, see N. N. Acharyya, *Historical Documents of Assam and Neighbouring States: Original Records in English* (New Delhi: Omsons, 1983), 53–68.

30. In *The Opium War, 1840–1842* (Chapel Hill: University of North Carolina Press, 1975), Peter Ward Fay writes, "Private merchants, not the Company, brought [opium] to China, but that made no difference; the Company, with its international reach, could obtain the dollars the drug earned by offering in exchange its bills payable in India or England" (54).

31. P. C. Kuo, *A Critical Study of the First Anglo-Chinese War* (1933; reprint, Westport, CT: Hyperion, 1973), 29.

32. Kuo, *Critical Study,* 108.

33. For a reading of the contradictions inherent in the idea of "wastelands," see Piya Chatterjee, *A Time for Tea: Women, Labor, and Post/Colonial Politics on an Indian Plantation* (Durham: Duke University Press, 2001), 63–70.

34. Priyam Goswami, *Assam in the Nineteenth Century: Industrialisation and Colonial Penetration* (Guwahati: Spectrum, 1999), 68.

35. Goswami, *Assam in the Nineteenth Century,* 76.

36. "Cultivation of the Tea-Plant in Assam," no. 1, *Penny Magazine* 9, no. 505 (February 15, 1840), 59.

37. "Cultivation of the Tea-Plant in Assam," 59.

38. E. P. Thompson, *The Making of the English Working Class* (New York: Vintage, 1966), 63.

39. Tea production may be classified as both agriculture and industry. See Gangadhar Banerjee, *Tea Plantation Industry between 1850 and 1992: Structural Changes* (Guwahati: Lawyer's Book Stall, 1996), chapter 3.

40. Michael Feldberg, "Knight's Penny Magazine and Chambers' Edinburgh Journal: A Problem in Writing Cultural History," *Victorian Periodicals Newsletter* 3 (1968): 13, 14. For a trenchant examination of the rhetoric of working-class temperance, see Deborah Mutch, "Intemperate Narratives: Tory Tipplers, Liberal Abstainers, and Victorian British Socialist Fiction," *Victorian Literature and Culture* 36 (2008): 471–87.

41. Ranajit Guha, "The Prose of Counter-Insurgency," in *Selected Subaltern Studies,* ed. Guha and Gayatri Chakravorty Spivak (New York: Oxford University Press, 1988), 77.

42. Rajnarayan Chandavarkar discusses the difficulties of reading an Indian "working class" through a British model in his essay "'The Making of the Working Class': E. P. Thompson and Indian History," in *Mapping Subaltern Studies and the Postcolonial,* ed. Vinayak Chaturvedi (London: Verso, 2000).

43. See Fromer, *A Necessary Luxury,* for a discussion of Robert Fortune's claim that tea cultivation would "civilize" South Asian workers by "giving them access to some of the luxuries currently available to the English middle classes" (63).

44. William Cobbett, *Cottage Economy* (London: C. Clement, 1822), 19–20.

45. This is not to say that its stimulant qualities went unrecognized; Cobbett calls it "a weaker kind of laudanum, which enlivens for the moment and deadens afterward" (13).

46. "Indian Teas and Chinese Travellers," 90.

47. "Indian Teas and Chinese Travellers," 95.

48. See Fromer, *A Necessary Luxury,* 12–13, 116–78, for a discussion of tea's relationship to class and gender boundaries.

49. Disraeli, *Sybil,* 120–21.

50. "Indian Teas and Chinese Travellers," 88.

51. Disraeli, *Sybil,* 121.

52. Elizabeth Gaskell, *Mary Barton* (Oxford: Oxford University Press, 1987), 13–14. For a fascinating reading of japan-ware in an 1880 Lipton tea advertisement, see Fromer, *A Necessary Luxury,* 83–85. See also my discussion of japan-ware in chapter 5.

53. Gaskell, *Mary Barton,* 16–17.

54. One of the first articulations of this line of criticism is Raymond Williams's chapter "The Industrial Novels" in *Culture and Society, 1780–1950* (1958;

New York: Columbia University Press, 1983); much earlier, Humphry House's chapter titled "Benevolence" in *The Dickens World* (2nd ed.; London: Oxford University Press, 1942) gestures at something similar. See also Martin Dodsworth's introduction to the Penguin edition of Gaskell's *North and South* (New York: Penguin, 1986). He writes, "It is a human understanding, rather than a political or economic understanding, that informs the whole novel" (20). In *The Novel and the Police*, D. A. Miller notes that in Dickens, "to witness the horror of the carceral [defined as the factory as well as the prison and the workhouse] was always to incur a debt of gratitude for the immunities of middle-class life" (59).

55. "Assam and the Hill Tribes" (*New Monthly Magazine* 80 [1847]), 308, 310. The essay claims that Assam is populated with "hardy, wild, and fierce tribes, among whom are to be found—as for example, among the hideous Nagas, who go naked, tatoo [*sic*] their skins, expose their dead, and eat reptiles and vermin—some probably of the most savage human beings to be found on the whole face of the earth" (308). It goes on to describe "the Khamtis," who "are addicted to opium and habitual indolence, are intelligent, vindictive, and cruel, [and] averse to regular labour," and "the Muttucks, a rude, fanatical, stiff-necked people" (311), among others.

56. "Tea," *Chambers's Journal* 36 (1861): 293.

57. "Indian Teas and Chinese Travellers," 89–90.

58. See, for example, Erika Rappaport's *Shopping for Pleasure: Women in the Making of London's West End* (Princeton: Princeton University Press, 2001), 74, on the rise of private women's clubs, in which members could socialize, drink tea, and attend lectures, debates, and concerts.

59. Charlotte Brontë, *Jane Eyre* (New York: Penguin, 2003), 84–85.

60. Brontë, *Jane Eyre*, 85.

61. Brontë, *Jane Eyre*, 85.

62. In "Three Women's Texts and a Critique of Imperialism," Spivak writes, "It is the unquestioned ideology of imperialist axiomatics . . . that conditions Jane's move from the counter-family set to the set of the family-in-law" (267); Bertha must "set fire to the house and kill herself, so that Jane Eyre can become the feminist individualist heroine of British fiction" (270).

63. Esther Summerson's household keys are mentioned frequently in *Bleak House;* one of the keys that Victorian women kept on their person was that of the tea caddy. Servants were not generally allowed unlimited access to tea, although they often had the privilege of drying their employers' used tea leaves to drink or to sell. Used tea leaves were also used for cleaning. See Henry Mayhew, "On the Hawking of Tea-Leaves," in *London Labour and the London Poor,* vol. 2 (London: Griffen, Bohn and Company, 1851). See also Fromer, *A Necessary Luxury,* 90–98, on the significance of preparing tea oneself as opposed to allowing servants to prepare it.

64. Charles Dickens, *The Old Curiosity Shop* (London: Penguin, 1985), 48.

65. Charles Dickens, *Bleak House* (New York: Penguin, 1985), 347.

66. *Oxford English Dictionary,* s.v. *slops.*

67. Daniel Bivona has observed that the Mad Hatter's tea party in *Alice's Adventures in Wonderland* is barely a tea party in any sense and "can only be yoked by violence to the English conception" (60); his larger argument calls into question the existence of the grounds of such a conception in the first place. So it is with most novelistic representations of tea drinking; as with the Smallweeds' tea, all seem to refer to a norm that is scarcely anywhere to be found.

68. Dickens, *Bleak House,* 496.

69. Dickens, *Bleak House,* 545.

70. Another example: in chapter 24 of Charlotte Brontë's *Shirley* (New York: Penguin, 1985), Caroline's uncle makes her first cup of tea himself as she emerges from a life-threatening illness (406).

71. Dickens, *Bleak House,* 389, 390.

72. Dickens, *Bleak House,* 915.

73. For another discussion of the "giving away" of Charley and Esther, see Timothy Peltason, "Esther's Will," *ELH* 59 (1991): 671–91. In *The Servant's Hand: English Fiction from Below* (Durham: Duke University Press, 1993), Bruce Robbins's reading of Hortense as Esther's surrogate in *Bleak House* productively complicates Esther's place in the servant-mistress binary (154–55).

74. For a discussion of "the connotative linkage of the erotics of femininity with the commodity and its assimilation to the structure of commodity fetishism," see Abigail Solomon-Godeau, "The Other Side of Venus: The Visual Economy of Feminine Display," in *The Sex of Things,* ed. de Grazia, 114. See also McClintock, *Imperial Leather,* chapter 3.

75. John Tosh, *A Man's Place: Masculinity and the Middle Class Home in Victorian England* (New Haven: Yale University Press, 2007). See especially chapter 2, "The Ideal of Domesticity."

76. "Indian Teas and Chinese Travellers," 88.

77. Dickens, *Bleak House,* 915.

78. Dickens, *Bleak House,* 116.

79. J. Sheridan LeFanu, "Green Tea," *Best Ghost Stories of J. S. LeFanu,* ed. E. F. Bleiler (New York: Dover, 1964), 192.

80. LeFanu, "Green Tea," 192 (emphasis in original).

81. LeFanu, "Green Tea," 192.

82. LeFanu, "Green Tea," 186.

83. LeFanu, "Green Tea," 181.

84. LeFanu, "Green Tea," 206–7.

85. LeFanu, "Green Tea," 206.

86. LeFanu, "Green Tea," 208–9.

87. J. Sheridan LeFanu, "Carmilla," *Best Ghost Stories of J. S. LeFanu,* ed. E. F. Bleiler (New York: Dover, 1964), 285.

88. W. J. McCormack, *Sheridan LeFanu* (Phoenix Mill: Sutton, 1997), 24.

89. Thomas De Quincey, *Confessions of an English Opium Eater and Other Writings,* ed. Aileen Ward (New York: Signet Classics, 1966), 73.

90. De Quincey, *Confessions of an English Opium Eater*, 78.

91. De Quincey, *Confessions of an English Opium Eater*, 80 (emphasis in original).

92. De Quincey, *Confessions of an English Opium Eater*, 94, 95.

93. The linked images of the "Malay" and opium will recur in Arthur Conan Doyle's story "The Man with the Twisted Lip" in *The Adventures of Sherlock Holmes*.

94. See Barbara T. Gates, "Blue Devils and Green Tea: Sheridan Le Fanu's Haunted Suicides," *Studies in Short Fiction* 24 (1987), for a discussion of these images in terms of being driven to suicide.

95. Little of the opium grown in India was exported to England. For the sources of opium consumed in England in the nineteenth century, and a sense of the dimensions of the international opium trade, see Virginia Berridge and Griffith Edwards, *Opium and the People: Opiate Use in Nineteenth-Century England* (New Haven: Yale University Press, 1987), 272–73.

CHAPTER 5

1. See Mehta, "English Romance; Indian Violence," for a thorough treatment of the connections between *The Moonstone* and *The Sign of Four*.

2. For an enlightening collection of fin de siècle descriptions of London, see appendix A to Julian Wolfreys's Broadview edition of Richard Marsh's *The Beetle* (Peterborough, Ontario: Broadview, 2004). *The Beetle,* published in 1897, features a malevolent and magical "Arab" who lives in a similar suburban wasteland in a house full of "Eastern curiosities" (260).

3. The figure of Count Dracula has been linked to anti-Semitic fear of eastern European Jews by Judith Halberstam; see *Skin Shows: Gothic Horror and the Technology of Monsters* (Durham: Duke University Press, 1995), chapter 4, especially 86–88, 91–93.

4. Yumna Siddiqi, "The Cesspool of Empire: Sherlock Holmes and the Return of the Repressed," *Victorian Literature and Culture* 34 (2006): 233. Siddiqi continues: "One, a contorted and bilious ex-soldier, owns a pet Indian mongoose. Another has lost a leg to a crocodile in the Ganges and has a poison-toting Andaman Islander in tow. A third keeps a fiendish hound and passes his South American wife off as his sister. A fourth returns from South Africa with a 'blanched' face and a furtive manner. . . . In actual fact, return from the colonies to the metropole was a routine phenomenon, and returned colonials were familiar figures on the metropolitan landscape."

5. Arthur Conan Doyle, *The Complete Sherlock Holmes* (New York: Barnes and Noble, 1992), 95.

6. Doyle, *The Sign of Four*, 99–100.

7. Doyle, *The Sign of Four*, 156.

8. Doyle, *The Sign of Four*, 100.

9. Christopher Keep and Don Randall, "Addiction, Empire, and Narrative in Arthur Conan Doyle's *The Sign of Four*," *Novel: A Forum on Fiction* 32 (1999): 213.

10. Keep and Randall, "Addiction, Empire, and Narrative," 214.

11. Doyle, *The Sign of Four*, 127, 128.

12. John McBratney, "Racial and Criminal Types: Indian Ethnography in Sir Arthur Conan Doyle's *The Sign of Four*," *Victorian Literature and Culture* 33 (2005): 155.

13. McBratney, "Racial and Criminal Types," 160.

14. Doyle, *The Sign of Four*, 89.

15. Doyle, *The Sign of Four*, 92.

16. Doyle, *The Sign of Four*, 94.

17. Doyle, *The Sign of Four*, 138.

18. See Gauri Viswanathan, "The Ordinary Business of Occultism," in *Critical Inquiry* 27 (2000), for a reading of the uses to which a mystical view of "Eastern spirituality" was put by Theosophists in the later nineteenth century.

19. Oscar Wilde, *The Picture of Dorian Gray* (New York: Norton, 2007), 5.

20. Wilde, *Dorian Gray*, 6.

21. Wilde, *Dorian Gray*, 5.

22. See Matt Cook, *London and the Culture of Homosexuality, 1885–1914* (Cambridge: Cambridge University Press, 2003), 107, for a reading of the homoerotic subtext of Henry's trip to a draper's shop in Wardour Street, Soho, where he bargains "for hours" for "a piece of old brocade" (*Dorian Gray*, 47).

23. Wilde, *Dorian Gray*, 23. Dorian repeats this phrase in chapter 16 as he seeks out an opium den after killing Basil Hallward (176).

24. Wilde, *Dorian Gray*, 27.

25. Talia Schaffer, "Craft, Authorial Anxiety, and 'The Cranford Papers,'" *Victorian Periodicals Review* 38 (2005): 222. Schaffer describes middle-class women around midcentury as having been "particularly taken with the exciting idea of gluing down shells, hair, sand, paper scraps, dried plants, or moss. In this new craze, natural objects were gilded, shellacked, wrapped in foil, dipped in wax, pierced, glued together, wrapped in fabric, or incorporated into a larger geometrical patterns. . . . Typical domestic handicrafts included wax fruit under glass, beaded bags, embroidered slippers, seaweed collages, shell-encrusted boxes, woolwork cushions, painted china, woven workbaskets, scrap screens, and satin pincushions" (221–22). Thus Basil's tea table and the Bartons' tea tray may be said to represent antithetical value-systems even as they serve much the same domestic purpose. See Frederick W. Burgess, *Antique Furniture* (New York: G. P. Putnam's Sons, 1915), 283–85, for an overview of British lacquer work, including japanning.

26. Toshio Yokoyama, *Japan in the Victorian Mind: A Study of Stereotyped Images of a Nation, 1850–80* (Houndsmills, Basingstoke: Macmillan, 1987), 5.

27. Yokoyama, *Japan in the Victorian Mind*, 116–24.

28. Cyprian Arthur George Bridge, "The City of Kiyôto." *Fraser's Magazine,* n.s., 17 (1878): 65.

29. Oscar Wilde, "The Decay of Lying," in *The Artist as Critic: Critical Writings of Oscar Wilde,* ed. Richard Ellmann (Chicago: University of Chicago Press, 1982), 299.

30. Wilde, "The Decay of Lying," 300.

31. Wilde, "The Decay of Lying," 301.

32. Wilde, "The Decay of Lying," 300.

33. Wilde, "The Decay of Lying," 303.

34. Wilde, "The Decay of Lying," 315.

35. Wilde, "The Decay of Lying," 315.

36. Wilde, "The Decay of Lying," 316.

37. Wilde, *Dorian Gray,* 21.

38. Dowling's *Hellenism and Homosexuality* is invaluable here. See also Cook, *London,* 33–34, 122–42, for a discussion of Hellenism in late-Victorian London and London as "Hellenic city," respectively.

39. Wilde, *Dorian Gray,* 37.

40. This is more or less the current critical consensus, although the novel's actual author(s) have not been definitively identified. See Cook, *London,* 104; Robert Gray and Christopher Keep, "'An Uninterrupted Current': Homoeroticism and Collaborative Authorship in *Teleny,*" in *Literary Couplings: Writing Couples, Collaborators, and the Construction of Authorship,* ed. Marjorie Stone and Judith Thompson (Madison: University of Wisconsin Press, 2006), 194–95.

41. Anonymous, *Teleny, or the Reverse of the Medal* (Ware, Hertfordshire: Wordsworth, 1995), 113 (emphasis in original).

42. *Teleny,* 114.

43. *Teleny,* 114–15.

44. Gray and Keep, "'An Uninterrupted Current,'" 197.

45. See Robert Aldrich, *Colonialism and Homosexuality* (London: Routledge, 2003), chapter 5, "Artists and Homoerotic 'Orientalism,'" chapter 9, "The British (and others) in South Asia," and chapter 11, "The French in North Africa," in which he recounts an 1895 meeting between André Gide, Oscar Wilde, and Alfred Douglas in Algeria. See also Anjali Arondekar, *For the Record: On Sexuality and the Colonial Archive in India* (Durham: Duke University Press, 2009). While Arondekar is more concerned to theorize and critique archival work in that she reads the colonial archive as incapable of bodying forth "lost" or "hidden" subjects in any uncomplicated manner, her own readings of the colonial archive also demonstrate the real-world coordinates of this fantasy even as she rigorously insists on "disorienting the teleological promise of archival claims" (17).

46. See, for example, Jonathan Gould, *Can't Buy Me Love: The Beatles, Britain, and America* (New York: Random House, 2008), 465–67, for a description of the Beatles' 1968 stay at the Maharishi Mahesh Yogi's ashram in Bishikesh.

Works Cited

"Accessions and Notes." *Metropolitan Museum of Art Bulletin* 20, no. 3 (March 1925): 85–88.

Acharyya, N. N. *Historical Documents of Assam and Neighbouring States: Original Records in English.* New Delhi: Omsons, 1983.

Achaya, K. T. *The Food Industries of British India.* Delhi: Oxford University Press, 1994.

Adburgham, Alison. *Shops and Shopping, 1800–1914: Where, and In What Manner the Well-dressed Englishwoman Bought Her Clothes.* London: George Allen and Unwin, 1964.

Aldrich, Robert. *Colonialism and Homosexuality.* London: Routledge, 2003.

Ames, Frank. *The Kashmir Shawl and Its Indo-French Influence.* Woodbridge, Suffolk: Antique Collectors' Club, 1997.

Anderson, Benedict. *Imagined Communities: Reflections on the Origin and Spread of Nationalism.* Rev. ed. London: Verso, 1991.

Appadurai, Arjun, ed. *The Social Life of Things: Commodities in Cultural Perspective.* Cambridge: Cambridge University Press, 1986.

Archer, Mildred. *Tippoo's Tiger.* London: H.M. Stationery Office, 1959.

Armstrong, Nancy. *Desire and Domestic Fiction: A Political History of the Novel.* New York: Oxford University Press, 1987.

Arondekar, Anjali. *For the Record: On Sexuality and the Colonial Archive in India.* Durham: Duke University Press, 2009.

"Assam and the Hill Tribes." *New Monthly Magazine* 80 (1847): 308–12.

Austen, Jane. *Works.* 6 volumes. Vol. 3, *Mansfield Park.* Ed. R. W. Chapman. Oxford: Oxford University Press, 1988.

Austen, Jane. *Works.* 6 volumes. Vol. 6, *Minor Works.* Ed. R. W. Chapman. Oxford: Oxford University Press, 1988.

Babu, T. M. *Diamonds in India.* Bangalore: Geological Society of India, 1998.

Badowska, Eva. "Choseville: Brontë's *Villette* and the Art of Bourgeois Interiority." *PMLA* 120 (2005): 1509–23.

Banerjee, Gangadhar. *Tea Plantation Industry between 1850 and 1992: Structural Changes.* Guwahati: Lawyer's Book Stall, 1996.

Barpujari, H. K. *Assam in the Days of the Company (1826–1858).* Gauhati, Assam: Spectrum, 1980.

Barpujari, H. K. *The Comprehensive History of Assam.* Vol. 5, *Modern Period: Yandabo to Diarchy, 1826–1919 A.D.* Guwahati: Publication Board Assam, 1990.

Barringer, Tim, and Tom Flynn. Editors' Introduction. *Colonialism and the Object: Empire, Material Culture, and the Museum.* London: Routledge, 1998.

Barthes, Roland. *Mythologies.* Trans. Annette Lavers. New York: Hill and Wang, 1972.

Bayly, C. A. "The Origins of Swadeshi (Home Industry): Cloth and Indian Society, 1700–1930." In *The Social Life of Things: Commodities in Cultural Perspective,* ed. Arjun Appadurai. Cambridge: Cambridge University Press, 1986.

Beeton, Mrs. *Mrs. Beeton's Book of Household Management.* London: S. O. Beeton, 1861.

Benson, Arthur Christopher, and Viscount Esher, eds. *The Letters of Queen Victoria.* Vol. 1. New York: Longmans, Green, 1907.

Berridge, Virginia, and Griffith Edwards. *Opium and the People: Opiate Use in Nineteenth-Century England.* New Haven: Yale University Press, 1987.

Bhabha, Homi K. "The World and the Home." In *Dangerous Liaisons: Gender, Nation, and Postcolonial Perspectives,* ed. Anne McClintock, Aamir Mufti, and Ella Shohat. Minneapolis: University of Minnesota Press, 1997.

Bhatia, Nandi. "Fashioning Women in Colonial India." *Fashion Theory* 7 (2003): 327–44.

Bivona, Daniel. *Desire and Contradiction: Imperial Visions and Domestic Debates in Victorian Literature.* Manchester: Manchester University Press, 1990.

Blunt, Alison. " 'The Flight from Lucknow': British Women Travelling and Writing Home, 1857–8." In *Writes of Passage: Reading Travel Writing,* ed. James Duncan and Derek Gregory. London: Routledge, 1999.

Bodenheimer, Rosemarie. *The Politics of Story in Victorian Social Fiction.* Ithaca: Cornell University Press, 1988.

Braddon, Mary Elizabeth. *Lady Audley's Secret.* 1862. New York: Oxford World's Classics, 1998.

Bramah Tea and Coffee Museum. *Guide and Souvenir Book.* London: Bramah Tea and Coffee Museum, 1997.

Brantlinger, Patrick. *Rule of Darkness: British Literature and Imperialism, 1830–1914.* Ithaca: Cornell University Press, 1988.

Bridge, Cyprian Arthur George. "The City of Kiyôto." *Fraser's Magazine,* n.s., 17 (1878): 58–70.

Brontë, Charlotte. *Jane Eyre.* 1847. New York: Penguin, 2003.

Brontë, Charlotte. *Shirley.* 1849. New York: Penguin, 1985.

Brontë, Charlotte. *Villette.* 1853. Oxford: Oxford University Press, 1990.

Brown, Bill. *The Material Unconscious: American Amusement, Stephen Crane, and the Economies of Play.* Cambridge: Harvard University Press, 1996.

Brown, Bill. *A Sense of Things: The Object Matter of American Literature.* Chicago: University of Chicago Press, 2003.

Buie, Sarah. "The Kashmir Shawl." *Asian Art and Culture* 9 (1996): 39–51.

Burgess, Frederick W. *Antique Furniture.* New York: G. P. Putnam's Sons, 1915.

Burton, Antoinette. *Burdens of History: British Feminists, Indian Women, and Imperial Culture, 1865–1915.* Chapel Hill: University of North Carolina Press, 1994.

Butler, John. *Travels and Adventures in the Province of Assam During a Residence of Fourteen Years.* 1855. Delhi: Vivek, 1978.

Carens, Timothy. *Outlandish English Subjects in the Victorian Domestic Novel.* Houndsmills, Basingstoke: Palgrave Macmillan, 2005.

"Cashmere Shawls: Of What Are They Made?" *Once a Week* 12 (January 1865): 68–70.

Chakrabarty, Dipesh. *Provincializing Europe: Postcolonial Thought and Historical Difference.* Princeton: Princeton University Press, 2000.

Chandavarkar, Rajnarayan. "'The Making of the Working Class': E. P. Thompson and Indian History." In *Mapping Subaltern Studies and the Postcolonial,* ed. Vinayak Chaturvedi. London: Verso, 2000.

Chandra, Bipan. *Essays on Colonialism.* Hyderabad: Orient Longman, 1999.

Chatterjee, Piya. *A Time for Tea: Women, Labor, and Post/Colonial Politics on an Indian Plantation.* Durham: Duke University Press, 2001.

Chaudhuri, Asim. *Enclaves in a Peasant Society: Political Economy of Tea in Western Dooars in Northern Bengal.* New Delhi: People's Publishing House, 1995.

Chaudhuri, K. N. *The Trading World of Asia and the English East India Company.* New York: Cambridge University Press, 1978.

Chaudhuri, Nupur. "Shawls, Jewelry, Curry, and Rice in Victorian Britain." In *Western Women and Imperialism: Complicity and Resistance,* ed. Nupur Chaudhuri and Margaret Strobel. Bloomington: Indiana University Press, 1992.

Chowdhury, Prosenjit. *Socio-Cultural Aspects of Assam in the Nineteenth Century.* New Delhi: Vikas, 1994.

Clabburn, Pamela. "British Shawls in the Indian Style." In *The Kashmir Shawl and Its Indo-French Influence,* ed. Frank Ames. Woodbridge, Suffolk: Antique Collectors' Club, 1997.

Cobbett, William. *Cottage Economy.* London: C. Clement, 1822.

Cockshut, A. O. J. *Anthony Trollope: A Critical Study.* London: Collins, 1955.

Cohen, William A. "Trollope's Trollop." *Novel* 28 (1995): 235–56.

Cohn, Bernard. "Cloth, Clothes, and Colonialism: India in the Nineteenth Century." In *Cloth and Human Experience,* ed. Annette B. Weiner and Jane Schneider. Washington, DC: Smithsonian Institution Press, 1989.

Collins, Wilkie. *Hide and Seek.* 1854. New York: Dover, 1981.

Collins, Wilkie. *The Moonstone.* 1868. Oxford: World's Classics, 1982.

Cook, Matt. *London and the Culture of Homosexuality, 1885–1914.* Cambridge: Cambridge University Press, 2003.

Copjec, Joan. *Read My Desire: Lacan Against the Historicists.* Cambridge: MIT Press, 1994.

Corrie, Rebecca Wells. "The Paisley." In *The Kashmir Shawl: Yale University Art Gallery, February 12–April 6, 1975.* New Haven: Yale University Art Gallery, 1975.

"Cotton." *Chambers's Journal* 19 (1863): 136–38.

"The Cotton Fields of India." *Dublin University Magazine* 49 (1857): 678–89.

"The Cotton Manufacture." *Westminster Review,* n.s., 19 (1861): 419–57.

"Cubbon, Sir Mark, 1784–1861." *Dictionary of National Biography on CD-ROM.* Version 1.0. Oxford: Oxford University Press, 1995.

"Cultivation of the Tea-Plant in Assam," no. 1. *Penny Magazine* 9, no. 505 (February 15, 1840): 59–60.

"Culture of Tea in the Himalayan Mountains." *Hogg's Weekly Instructor* (1852).

Dames, Nicholas. "The Clinical Novel: Phrenology and *Villette.*" *Novel* 29 (1996): 367–90.

David, Deirdre. *Rule Britannia: Women, Empire, and Victorian Writing.* Ithaca: Cornell University Press, 1995.

Davidoff, Leonore, and Catherine Hall. *Family Fortunes: Men and Women of the English Middle Class, 1780–1850.* Chicago: University of Chicago Press, 1987.

Davis, Nuel Pharr. *The Life of Wilkie Collins.* Urbana: University of Illinois Press, 1956.

De Almeida, Hermione, and George H. Gilpin. *Indian Renaissance: British Romantic Art and the Prospect of India.* Aldershot: Ashgate, 2006.

De Grazia, Victoria, ed., with Ellen Furlough. *The Sex of Things: Gender and Consumption in Historical Perspective.* Berkeley: University of California Press, 1996.

De Quincey, Thomas. *Confessions of an English Opium Eater and Other Writings.* 1821. Ed. Aileen Ward. New York: Signet Classics, 1966.

Dhar, D. N. *Socio-Economic History of Kashmir Peasantry.* Srinaghar, Kashmir: Centre for Kashmir Studies, 1989.

Dickens, Charles. *Bleak House.* 1853. New York: Penguin, 1985.

Dickens, Charles. *Martin Chuzzlewit.* 1844. New York: Penguin, 1999.

Dickens, Charles. *The Old Curiosity Shop.* 1841. London: Penguin, 1985.

Dickens, Charles. *Our Mutual Friend.* 1865. New York: Penguin Classics, 1997.

Dickerson, Vanessa D., ed. *Keeping the Victorian House: A Collection of Essays.* New York: Garland, 1995.

Disraeli, Benjamin. *Sybil, or the Two Nations.* 1845. Oxford: Oxford University Press, 1998.

Dodsworth, Martin. Introduction to *North and South,* by Elizabeth Gaskell. New York: Penguin, 1986.

Douglas, Mary, and Baron Isherwood. *The World of Goods: Toward an Anthropology of Consumption.* New York: W. W. Norton, 1979.

Dowling, Linda. *Hellenism and Homosexuality in Victorian Oxford.* Ithaca: Cornell University Press, 1994.

Dowling, Linda. *Language and Decadence in the Victorian Fin de Siècle.* Princeton: Princeton University Press, 1986.

Doyle, Arthur Conan. *The Complete Sherlock Holmes.* New York: Barnes and Noble, 1992.

Duncan, Ian. "The Moonstone, the Victorian Novel, and Imperialist Panic." *MLQ* 55 (1994): 297–319.

Dutta, Arup Kumar. *Cha Garam! The Tea Story.* Assam: Paloma, 1992.

Eliot, George. *The Mill on the Floss.* 1860. New York: Signet, 1981.

"An Extinct Art." *Magazine of Art* 25 (1901): 452–53.

Fanon, Frantz. *A Dying Colonialism.* Trans. Haakon Chevalier. New York: Grove, 1965.

Farwell, Byron. *Queen Victoria's Little Wars.* New York: Norton, 1972.

Fay, Peter Ward. *The Opium War, 1840–1842.* Chapel Hill: University of North Carolina Press, 1975.

Feldberg, Michael. "Knight's Penny Magazine and Chambers' Edinburgh Journal: A Problem in Writing Cultural History." *Victorian Periodicals Newsletter* 3 (1968): 13–16.

Flavin, Michael. *Benjamin Disraeli: The Novel as Political Discourse.* Brighton: Sussex Academic Press, 2005.

Forrest, Denys. *Tea for the British: The Social and Economic History of a Famous Trade.* London: Chatto and Windus, 1973.

Freedgood, Elaine. "'Fine Fingers': Victorian Handmade Lace and Utopian Consumption." *Victorian Studies* 45 (2003): 625–47.

Freedgood, Elaine. *The Ideas in Things: Fugitive Meaning in the Victorian Novel.* Chicago: University of Chicago Press, 2006.

Freud, Sigmund. *The Interpretation of Dreams.* 1899. Trans. James Strachey. New York: Avon, 1965.

Fromer, Julie. "'Deeply Indebted to the Tea-Plant': Representations of English National Identity in Victorian Histories of Tea." *Victorian Literature and Culture* 36 (2008): 531–47.

Fromer, Julie. *A Necessary Luxury: Tea in Victorian England.* Athens: Ohio University Press, 2008.

Gallagher, Catherine. *The Industrial Reformation of English Fiction: Social Discourse and Narrative Form, 1832–1867.* Chicago: University of Chicago Press, 1985.

Galt, John. *Annals of the Parish.* 1821. Edinburgh: Mercat, 1994.

Gaskell, Elizabeth. *Cranford/Cousin Phyllis.* 1853, 1863. New York: Penguin, 1986.

Gaskell, Elizabeth. *Mary Barton.* 1848. Oxford: Oxford University Press, 1987.

Gaskell, Elizabeth. *North and South.* 1851. New York: Penguin, 1995.

Gaskell, Elizabeth. *Ruth*. 1853. New York: Penguin, 2004.

Gaskell, Elizabeth. *Wives and Daughters*. 1866. New York: Penguin, 2001.

Gates, Barbara T. "Blue Devils and Green Tea: Sheridan Le Fanu's Haunted Suicides." *Studies in Short Fiction* 24 (1987): 15–23.

Gillow, John, and Nicholas Barnard. *Traditional Indian Textiles*. London: Thames and Hudson, 1991.

Goswami, Priyam. *Assam in the Nineteenth Century: Industrialisation and Colonial Penetration*. Guwahati: Spectrum, 1999.

Gould, Jonathan. *Can't Buy Me Love: The Beatles, Britain, and America*. New York: Random House, 2008.

Gray, Robert, and Christopher Keep. "'An Uninterrupted Current': Homoeroticism and Collaborative Authorship in *Teleny*." In *Literary Couplings: Writing Couples, Collaborators, and the Construction of Authorship*, ed. Marjorie Stone and Judith Thompson. Madison: University of Wisconsin Press, 2006.

Great Britain. Parliamentary Papers. Accounts and Papers: 1866, vol. 52.

Grewal, Inderpal. *Home and Harem: Nation, Gender, Empire, and the Cultures of Travel*. Durham: Duke University Press, 1996.

Guha, Amalendu. "Colonisation of Assam: Second Phase, 1840–1859." *Indian Economic and Social History Review* 4 (1967): 289–318.

Guha, Amalendu. *Planter-Raj to Swaraj: Freedom Struggle and Electoral Politics in Assam, 1826–1947*. New Delhi: Indian Council of Historical Research, 1977.

Guha, Ranajit. *Elementary Aspects of Peasant Insurgency in Colonial India*. 1983. Durham: Duke University Press, 1999.

Guha, Ranajit. *History at the Limit of World-History*. New York: Columbia University Press, 2002.

Guha, Ranajit. "The Prose of Counter-Insurgency." *Selected Subaltern Studies*, ed. Ranajit Guha and Gayatri Chakravorty Spivak. New York: Oxford University Press, 1988.

Halberstam, Judith. *Skin Shows: Gothic Horror and the Technology of Monsters*. Durham: Duke University Press, 1995.

Hall, Catherine. "'From Greenland's Icy Mountains . . . to Afric's Golden Sand': Ethnicity, Race, and Nation in Mid-Nineteenth-Century England." *Gender and History* 5 (1993): 212–30.

Hall, Catherine, ed. *Cultures of Empire: Colonizers in Britain and the Empire in the Nineteenth and Twentieth Centuries*. New York: Routledge, 2000.

Hall, Catherine, and Sonya O. Rose, eds. *At Home with the Empire: Metropolitan Culture and the Imperial World*. Cambridge: Cambridge University Press, 2006.

Hall, N. John, ed. *The Letters of Anthony Trollope*. 2 vols. Stanford: Stanford University Press, 1983.

Halperin, John. "The Eustace Diamonds and Politics." In *Anthony Trollope*, ed. Tony Bareham. London: Vision Press, 1980.

Hamilton, C. J. *The Trade Relations between England and India (1600–1896)*. 1919. Delhi: Idarah-I Adabiyat-I Delli, 1975.

Harlow, George E., ed. *The Nature of Diamonds*. Cambridge: Cambridge University Press, 1998.

Harnetty, Peter. *Imperialism and Free Trade: Lancashire and India in the Mid-Nineteenth Century*. Vancouver: University of British Columbia Press, 1972.

Harrison, Emily Leland. "Ancient Lace." *Bulletin of the Pennsylvania Museum* 3, no. 9 (1905): 1–5.

Hasseler, Terri A. "Mr. Punch's Crinoline Anxiety: The Indian Rebellion and the Rhetoric of Dress." In *Comedy, Fantasy, and Colonialism*, ed. Graeme Harper. London: Continuum, 2002.

Helland, Janice. "'Caprices of Fashion': Handmade Lace in Ireland, 1883–1907." *Textile History* 39 (2008): 193–222.

Heller, Tamar. *Dead Secrets: Wilkie Collins and the Female Gothic*. New Haven: Yale University Press, 1992.

House, Humphry. *The Dickens World*. 2nd ed. London: Oxford University Press, 1942.

Howell, Martha C. "Fixing Movables: Gifts by Testament in Late Medieval Douai." *Past and Present* 150 (1996): 3–45.

Hubel, Teresa. *Whose India? The Independence Struggle in British and Indian Fiction and History*. Durham: Duke University Press, 1996.

"Indian Cotton and Its Supply." *Cornhill Magazine* 6 (November 1862): 654–62.

"Indian Teas and Chinese Travellers." *Fraser's Magazine* 47 (January 1853): 88–99.

Irwin, John. *The Kashmir Shawl*. London: Her Majesty's Stationery Office, 1973.

Ives, Maura. "Housework, Mill Work, Women's Work: The Functions of Cloth in Charlotte Brontë's *Shirley*." In *Keeping the Victorian House: A Collection of Essays*, ed. Vanessa D. Dickerson. New York: Garland, 1995.

Jameson, Fredric. *The Modernist Papers*. London: Verso, 2007.

Jay, Elisabeth. Introduction to *Miss Marjoribanks*, by Margaret Oliphant. New York: Penguin, 1998.

Jones, Ann Rosalind, and Peter Stallybrass. *Renaissance Clothing and the Materials of Memory*. Cambridge: Cambridge University Press, 2000.

Kapur, Manohar Lal. *Social and Economic History of Jammu and Kashmir State, 1885–1925 A.D.* New Delhi: Anmol, 1992.

Keay, John. *The Honourable Company: A History of the English East India Company*. London: HarperCollins, 1991.

Keen, Suzanne. "Quaker Dress, Sexuality, and the Domestication of Reform in the Victorian Novel." *Victorian Literature and Culture* 30 (2002): 211–36.

Keep, Christopher, and Don Randall. "Addiction, Empire, and Narrative in Arthur Conan Doyle's *The Sign of Four*." *Novel: A Forum on Fiction* 32 (1999): 207–21.

Kipling, Rudyard. *The Jungle Books*. New York: Penguin, 1989.

Kowaleski-Wallace, Beth. "Tea, Gender, and Domesticity in Eighteenth-Century England." *Studies in Eighteenth-Century Culture* 23 (1994): 131–45.

Kucich, John. *Imperial Masochism: British Fiction, Fantasy, and Social Class.* Princeton: Princeton University Press, 2006.

Kuo, P. C. *A Critical Study of the First Anglo-Chinese War.* 1933. Reprint, Westport, CT: Hyperion, 1973.

Lamont, Claire. Historical Note to *The Surgeon's Daughter.* Scott, *Chronicles of the Canongate.* New York: Penguin, 2003.

Law, Graham. "Industrial Designs: Form and Function in the 'Condition-of-England' Novel." In *Corresponding Powers: Studies in Honor of Professor Hisaaki Yamanouchi,* ed. George Hughes. Cambridge: D. S. Brewer, 1997.

Lawson, Philip. *A Taste for Empire and Glory: Studies in British Overseas Expansion, 1660–1800.* Aldershot: Variorum/Ashgate, 1997.

Lee, Martyn J. *Consumer Culture Reborn: The Cultural Politics of Consumption.* London: Routledge, 1993.

LeFanu, J. Sheridan. *Best Ghost Stories of J. S. LeFanu.* Ed. E. F. Bleiler. New York: Dover, 1964.

Lemire, Beverly. *Fashion's Favourite: The Cotton Trade and the Consumer in Britain, 1660–1800.* Oxford: Oxford University Press, 1991.

Levinson, Alfred A. "Diamond Sources and Their Discovery." In *The Nature of Diamonds,* ed. George E. Harlow. Cambridge: Cambridge University Press, 1998.

Lévi-Strauss, Monique. *The Cashmere Shawl.* Trans. Sara Harris. New York: Harry N. Abrams, 1988.

Lincoln, Andrew. *Walter Scott and Modernity.* Edinburgh: Edinburgh University Press, 2007.

Lindner, Christoph. *Fictions of Commodity Culture.* Aldershot, Hampshire: Ashgate, 2003.

Makdisi, Saree. *Romantic Imperialism: Universal Empire and the Culture of Modernity.* Cambridge: Cambridge University Press, 1998.

"Making Tea in India." *All The Year Round* (1864).

Mani, Lata. *Contentious Traditions: The Debate on Sati in Colonial India.* Berkeley: University of California Press, 1998.

Marsh, Richard. *The Beetle.* 1897. Ed. Julian Wolfreys. Peterborough, Ont.: Broadview, 2004.

Martineau, Harriet. "Shawls." *Household Words* 5, no. 127 (August 28, 1852): 552–56.

Marx, Karl. *Capital: A Critique of Political Economy.* Vol. 1. Trans. Ben Fowkes. New York: Penguin, 1990.

Marx, Karl. *Grundrisse: Foundations of the Critique of Political Economy.* Trans. Martin Nicolaus. New York: Penguin, 1993.

Marx, Karl. *The Political and Philosophical Manuscripts of 1844.* Trans. Martin Milligan. Ed. Dirk J. Struik. New York: International, 1964.

Marx, Karl. *Surveys From Exile: Political Writings.* Vol. 2. Ed. David Fernbach. London: Penguin, 1992.

Marx, Karl. "Whose Atrocities?" 1857. *Marx/Engels WWW Archive.* http://www .marxists.org/archive/marx/works/1857/04/10.htm.

Marx, Karl, and Friedrich Engels. "The Communist Manifesto." Trans. S. Moore. In *The Portable Karl Marx,* ed. Eugene Kamenka. New York: Viking Penguin, 1983.

Mayhew, Henry. *London Labour and the London Poor.* Vol. 2. London: Griffen, Bohn, and Company, 1851.

McBratney, John. "Racial and Criminal Types: Indian Ethnography in Sir Arthur Conan Doyle's *The Sign of Four.*" *Victorian Literature and Culture* 33 (2005): 149–67.

McClintock, Anne. *Imperial Leather: Race, Gender, and Sexuality in the Colonial Contest.* New York: Routledge, 1995.

McClintock, Anne, Aamir Mufti, and Ella Shohat, eds. *Dangerous Liaisons: Gender, Nation, and Postcolonial Perspectives.* Minneapolis: University of Minnesota Press, 1997.

McCormack, W. J. Introduction to *The Eustace Diamonds,* by Anthony Trollope. Oxford: Oxford University Press, 1983.

McCormack, W. J. *Sheridan LeFanu.* 1980. Phoenix Mill: Sutton, 1997.

Mehta, Jaya. "English Romance; Indian Violence." *Centennial Review* 34 (1995): 611–57.

Meyer, Susan. *Imperialism at Home: Race and Victorian Women's Fiction.* Ithaca: Cornell University Press, 1996.

Miller, Andrew H. *Novels Behind Glass: Commodity Culture and Victorian Narrative.* Cambridge: Cambridge University Press, 1995.

Miller, D. A. *Jane Austen, or The Secret of Style.* Princeton: Princeton University Press, 2003.

Miller, D. A. *The Novel and the Police.* Berkeley: University of California Press, 1988.

Milligan, Barry. *Pleasures and Pains: Opium and the Orient in Nineteenth-Century British Culture.* Charlottesville: University of Virginia Press, 1995.

Moretti, Franco. *Atlas of the European Novel, 1800–1900.* London: Verso, 1998.

Moretti, Franco. *The Way of the World: The Bildungsroman in European Culture.* London: Verso, 2000.

"Morley, John, Viscount Morley of Blackburn, 1838–1923." *Dictionary of National Biography on CD-ROM.* Version 1.0. Oxford: Oxford University Press, 1995.

Mozley, Anne. "Dress." *Blackwood's Magazine* 57 (April 1865): 425–38.

Mufti, Aamir, and Ella Shohat. Introduction. In *Dangerous Liaisons: Gender, Nation, and Postcolonial Perspectives,* ed. Anne McClintock, Aamir Mufti, and Ella Shohat. Minneapolis: University of Minnesota Press, 1997.

Mukherjee, Ramkrishna. *The Rise and Fall of the East India Company: A Sociological Appraisal.* New York: Monthly Review Press, 1974.

Mukherjee, Upamanyu Pablo. *Crime and Empire: The Colony in Nineteenth-Century Fictions of Crime.* Oxford: Oxford University Press, 2003.

Mukherji, Chandra. *From Graven Images: Patterns of Modern Materialism.* New York: Columbia University Press, 1983.

Munich, Adrienne. *Queen Victoria's Secrets.* New York: Columbia University Press, 1996.

Murthy, H. V. Sreenivasa, and R. Ramakrishnan. *A History of Karnataka (From the Earliest Times to the Present Day).* New Delhi: S. Chand, 1977.

Mutch, Deborah. "Intemperate Narratives: Tory Tipplers, Liberal Abstainers, and Victorian British Socialist Fiction." *Victorian Literature and Culture* 36 (2008): 471–87.

Oliphant, Margaret. *Hester.* 1883. New York: Penguin/Virago, 1984.

Oliphant, Margaret. *Miss Marjoribanks.* 1866. New York: Penguin, 1998.

O'Mealy, Joseph H. "Mrs. Oliphant, *Miss Marjoribanks* (1866), and the Victorian Canon." In *The New Nineteenth Century: Feminist Readings of Underread Victorian Novels,* ed. Barbara Leah Harmon and Susan Meyer. New York: Garland, 1996.

Panigrahi, Tara Sankar. *The British Rule and the Economy of Rural Bengal: A Study of Mallabhum from 1757 to 1833.* New Delhi: Marwah, 1982.

Pauley, Sarah Buie. "The Shawl: Its Context and Construction." *The Kashmir Shawl: Yale University Art Gallery, February 12–April 6, 1975.* New Haven: Yale University Art Gallery, 1975.

Peltason, Timothy. "Esther's Will." *ELH* 59 (1991): 671–91.

Perera, Suvendrini. *Reaches of Empire: The English Novel from Edgeworth to Dickens.* New York: Columbia University Press, 1991.

Plotz, John. *Portable Property: Victorian Culture on the Move.* Princeton: Princeton University Press, 2008.

Plumptre, Annabella. *Domestic Management; or, the Healthful Cookery-Book.* London: 1810.

Pointon, Marcia. "Intriguing Jewellery: Royal Bodies and Luxurious Consumption." *Textual Practice* 11 (1997): 493–516.

Poovaya-Smith, Nima. "Keys to the Magic Kingdom: The New Transcultural Collections of Bradford Art Galleries and Museums." In *Colonialism and the Object: Empire, Material Culture, and the Museum,* ed. Tim Barringer and Tom Flynn. London: Routledge, 1998.

Prakash, Gyan, ed. *After Colonialism: Imperial Histories and Postcolonial Displacements.* Princeton: Princeton University Press, 1995.

Préteceille, Edmond, and Jean-Pierre Terrail. *Capitalism, Consumption, and Needs.* Trans. Sarah Matthews. Oxford: Basil Blackwell, 1985.

Quayle, Eric. *Old Cook Books: An Illustrated History.* New York: Brandywine-E. P. Dutton, 1978.

Raina, N. N. *Kashmir Politics and Imperialist Manoeuvres, 1846–1980.* New Delhi: Patriot, 1988.

Rappaport, Erika. *Shopping for Pleasure: Women in the Making of London's West End.* Princeton: Princeton University Press, 2001.

Ray, Sangeeta. *En-Gendering India: Woman and Nation in Colonial and Postcolonial Narratives.* Durham: Duke University Press, 2000.

Reed, John R. "English Imperialism and the Unacknowledged Crime of *The Moonstone.*" *Clio* 2 (1973): 281–90.

Rehman, Sherry, and Naheed Jafri. *The Kashmiri Shawl: From Jamavar to Paisley.* Woodbridge, Suffolk: Antique Collectors' Club, 2006.

Ribeiro, Aileen. *The Art of Dress: Fashion in England and France, 1750–1820.* New Haven: Yale University Press, 1995.

Richards, Thomas. *The Commodity Culture of Victorian England: Advertising and Spectacle, 1851–1914.* Stanford: Stanford University Press, 1990.

Richardson, Ruth. *Death, Dissection, and the Destitute.* Chicago: University of Chicago Press, 2001.

Robbins, Bruce. *The Servant's Hand: English Fiction from Below.* Durham: Duke University Press, 1993.

Rosenblum, Robert. *Jean-Auguste-Dominique Ingres.* New York: Harry N. Abrams, 1986.

Rosenman, Ellen Bayuk. "More Stories about Clothing and Furniture: Realism and Bad Commodities." In *Functions of Victorian Culture at the Present Time,* ed. Christine Krueger. Athens: Ohio University Press, 2002.

Roy, Ashish. "The Fabulous Imperialist Semiotic of Wilkie Collins's The Moonstone." *New Literary History* 24 (1997): 657–81.

Roy, Parama. *Indian Traffic: Identities in Question in Colonial and Postcolonial India.* Berkeley: University of California Press, 1998.

Ruskin, John. *The Two Paths. Complete Works.* Vols. 11–12. New York: Thomas P. Crowell, 1909.

Said, Edward W. *Culture and Imperialism.* New York: Vintage, 1994.

Said, Edward W. *Orientalism.* New York: Vintage, 1979.

Schaffer, Talia. "Craft, Authorial Anxiety, and 'The Cranford Papers.'" *Victorian Periodicals Review* 38 (2005): 221–39.

Scott, Walter. *Chronicles of the Canongate.* 1828. Ed. Claire Lamont. London: Penguin, 2003.

Scott, Walter. *The Surgeon's Daughter.* Waverley novels vol. 20, *Chronicles of the Canongate.* First series. Boston: Sanborn, Carter, and Bazin, 1855.

Sever, Adrian, ed. *Documents and Speeches on the Indian Princely States.* Vol. 1. Delhi: B. R. Publishing, 1985.

Sharpe, Jenny. *Allegories of Empire: The Figure of Woman in the Colonial Text.* Minneapolis: University of Minnesota Press, 1993.

Siddiqi, Yumna. "The Cesspool of Empire: Sherlock Holmes and the Return of the Repressed." *Victorian Literature and Culture* 34 (2006): 233–47.

Silver, Arthur. *Manchester Men and Indian Cotton, 1847–1872.* Manchester: Manchester University Press, 1966.

Sinha, N. K. *Economic History of Bengal.* 3 vols. Calcutta: Firma K. L. Mukhopad-hyay, 1956–70.

Skilton, David. *Anthony Trollope and His Contemporaries: A Study in the Theory and Conventions of Mid-Victorian Fiction.* New York: St. Martin's, 1996.

Solomon-Godeau, Abigail. "The Other Side of Venus: The Visual Economy of Feminine Display." In *The Sex of Things: Gender and Consumption in Historical Perspective,* ed. Victoria de Grazia with Ellen Furlough. Berkeley: University of California Press, 1996.

Spivak, Gayatri Chakravorty. *A Critique of Postcolonial Reason: Toward a History of the Vanishing Present.* Cambridge: Harvard University Press, 1999.

Spivak, Gayatri Chakravorty. "Three Women's Texts and a Critique of Imperialism." In *"Race," Writing, and Difference,* ed. Henry Louis Gates. Chicago: University of Chicago Press, 1986.

Stallybrass, Peter. "Marx's Coat." In *Border Fetishisms: Material Objects in Unstable Spaces,* ed. Patricia Spyer. New York: Routledge, 1998.

Stone, Elizabeth. *William Langshawe, The Cotton Lord.* London: Richard Bentley, 1842.

Sunder Rajan, Rajeswari. *Real and Imagined Women: Gender, Culture, and Postcolonialism.* London: Routledge, 1993.

Swedenborg, Emanuel. *Arcana Celestia.* 12 vols. Vol. 4. 1751. Trans. and ed. John Faulkner Potts. New York: Swedenborg Foundation, 1984.

Swedenborg, Emanuel. *Arcana Celestia.* 12 vols. Vol. 7. 1753. Trans. and ed. John Faulkner Potts. New York: Swedenborg Foundation, 1978.

Taylor, Philip Meadows. "Indian Costumes and Textile Fabrics." *Edinburgh Review* 126 (July 1867): 125–50.

"Tea." *Chambers's Journal* 36 (1861): 293–96.

"The Tea-Plant." *Hogg's Weekly Instructor* (1846).

"Teas and the Tea Country." *New Monthly Magazine* 9 (August 1852): 76–89.

Teleny, or the Reverse of the Medal. Ware, Hertfordshire: Wordsworth, 1995.

Thackeray, William. *The History of Pendennis.* 1850. Oxford: Oxford World's Classics, 1994.

Thackeray, William. *Vanity Fair.* 1848. Oxford: Oxford University Press, 1983.

Thompson, E. P. *The Making of the English Working Class.* New York: Vintage, 1966.

Tosh, John. *A Man's Place: Masculinity and the Middle-Class Home in Victorian England.* New Haven: Yale University Press, 2007.

"Travel and Adventures in the Province of Assam." *New Quarterly Review* (1855).

Trollope, Anthony. *Autobiography.* 1883. London: Penguin, 1996.

Trollope, Anthony. *The Eustace Diamonds.* 1872. Oxford: Oxford University Press, 1983.

Ukers, William H. *All About Tea.* Vol. 2. New York: Tea and Coffee Trade Journal Company, 1935.

Untracht, Oppi. *Traditional Jewelry of India.* New York: Harry N. Abrams, 1997.

U.S. Customs Today online 38, no. 5 (May 2002). United States Customs and Border Protection. http://www.cbp.gov/xp/CustomsToday/2002/May/shahtoosh .xml.

Valverde, Mariana. "The Love of Finery: Fashion and the Fallen Woman in Nineteenth-Century Discourse." *Victorian Studies* 32 (1989): 169–88.

Vigne, Georges. *Ingres.* Trans. John Goodman. New York: Abbeville Press, 1995.

"A Visit to Cashmere, by a Captain in Her Majesty's Service." *Fraser's,* n.s., 8 (July 1873).

Visram, Rozina. *Asians in Britain: 400 Years of History.* London: Pluto, 2002.

Viswanathan, Gauri. *Masks of Conquest: Literary Study and British Rule in India.* 1989. Reprint. Delhi: Oxford University Press, 1998.

Viswanathan, Gauri. "The Ordinary Business of Occultism." *Critical Inquiry* 27 (2000): 1–20.

Viswanathan, Gauri. *Outside the Fold: Conversion, Modernity, and Belief.* Princeton: Princeton University Press, 1998.

Viswanathan, Gauri. "Raymond Williams and British Colonialism." *Yale Journal of Criticism* 4 (1991): 47–66.

Walkowitz, Judith R. *City of Dreadful Delight: Narratives of Sexual Danger in Late-Victorian London.* Chicago: University of Chicago Press, 1992.

Walkowitz, Judith R. *Prostitution and Victorian Society: Women, Class, and the State.* Cambridge: Cambridge University Press, 1980.

Wallerstein, Immanuel. *The Modern World-System III: The Second Era of Great Expansion of the Capitalist World-Economy, 1730–1840s.* San Diego: Academic Press, 1989.

Walter Scott Digital Archive. Edinburgh University. http://www.walterscott.lib.ed .ac.uk/works/novels/daughter.html.

Walton, Priscilla L. *Patriarchal Desire and Victorian Discourse: A Lacanian Reading of Anthony Trollope's Palliser Novels.* Toronto: University of Toronto Press, 1995.

Walvin, James. *Fruits of Empire: Exotic Produce and British Taste, 1660–1800.* New York: New York University Press, 1997.

Watson, J. Forbes. *The Textile Manufacturers and the Costumes of the People of India.* London, 1866.

Weiner, Annette B. "Cultural Difference and the Density of Objects." *American Ethnologist* 21 (1993): 391–403.

Weiner, Annette B., and Jane Schneider, eds. *Cloth and Human Experience.* Washington, DC: Smithsonian Institution Press, 1989.

Wellesley, Arthur. *Supplementary Despatches and Memoranda of Field Marshal Arthur Duke of Wellington, K.G.* Vol. 1. London: John Murray, 1858.

Wheeler, Michael. "Two Tales of Manchester Life." *Gaskell Society Journal* 3 (1989): 6–28.

White, Charles. *The Cashmere Shawl: An Eastern Fiction.* 3 vols. London: Henry Colburn, 1840.

Wilde, Oscar. *The Artist as Critic: Critical Writings of Oscar Wilde.* Ed. Richard Ell-
    mann. Chicago: University of Chicago Press, 1982.

Wilde, Oscar. *The Importance of Being Earnest and Other Plays.* Oxford: Oxford
    University Press, 1998.

Wilde, Oscar. *The Picture of Dorian Gray.* New York: Norton, 2007.

Wilde, Oscar. *A Woman of No Importance.* London: A & C Black, 1993.

Williams, Raymond. *The Country and the City.* New York: Oxford University
    Press, 1975.

Williams, Raymond. *Culture and Society, 1780–1950.* 1958. New York: Columbia
    University Press, 1983.

Yokoyama, Toshio. *Japan in the Victorian Mind: A Study of Stereotyped Images of a
    Nation 1850–80.* Houndsmills, Basingstoke: Macmillan, 1987.

Yonge, Charlotte. *The Clever Woman of the Family.* 1865. New York: Penguin/Vi-
    rago, 1986.

Young, Robert. *Colonial Desire: Hybridity in Theory, Culture, and Race.* London:
    Routledge, 1995.

Youngkin, Molly. "'Into the Woof, A Little Thibet Wool': Orientalism and Rep-
    resenting 'Reality' in Walter Scott's *The Surgeon's Daughter.*" *Scottish Studies
    Review* 3 (2002): 33–57.

Zizek, Slavoj. *The Sublime Object of Ideology.* London: Verso, 1989.

Zutshi, Chitralekha. "'Designed for Eternity': Kashmiri Shawls, Empire, and Cul-
    tures of Production and Consumption in Mid-Victorian Britain." *Journal of
    British Studies* 48 (2009): 420–40.

Index